ATLAS OF AOTEAROA NEW ZEALAND AND THE WORLD

hachette
AOTEAROA | NEW ZEALAND

Contents

World statistics: Countries 3

World statistics: Physical Dimensions 4

New Zealand Maps

New Zealand: Relief of Land 1:7 000 000 5

New Zealand: Physical Environment 6–7

New Zealand: Population 8–9

New Zealand: Economy 10–11

New Zealand: North Island 1:3 500 000 12

Wellington

New Zealand: South Island 1:3 500 000 13

Chatham Islands

Islands of the South-west Pacific 1:5 000 000 14

Fiji, Vanuatu, Solomon Islands, Tonga, Guam,

Tahiti and Moorea, Samoan Islands, New Caledonia

Index to New Zealand Maps 15–16

Table of reo Māori place names and world map 16

World Maps

Time Zones and Key to Map Symbols 1

The World: Physical 1:95 000 000 2–3

The World: Political 1:95 000 000 4–5

Polar Regions 1:35 000 000 6

Scandinavia and the Baltic Lands 1:10 000 000 7

Iceland

England and Wales 1:2 000 000 8–9

Scotland 1:2 000 000 10

Ireland 1:2 000 000 11

France 1:5 000 000 12

Spain and Portugal 1:5 000 000 13

Italy and the Balkan States 1:5 000 000 14–15

Germany and Central Europe 1:5 000 000 16

South-east Europe and Turkey 1:10 000 000 17

Russia and Northern Asia 1:20 000 000 18–19

China and the Far East 1:15 000 000 20–21

Hong Kong, Macau and Shenzhen

Japan 1:6 400 000 22

South-east Asia 1:20 000 000 23

Southern Asia and the Middle East 1:17 500 000 24–25

Northern Africa 1:15 000 000 26–27

Azores and Cape Verde Islands

Central and Southern Africa 1:15 000 000 28–29

Madagascar, Seychelles, Réunion, Mauritius and Comoros

Australia and Oceania 1:20 000 000 30–31

South-east Australia 1:8 000 000 32

Tasmania

New Zealand 1:6 000 000 33

Fiji, Tonga, Samoan Islands, Tahiti and Moorea

Pacific Ocean 1:54 000 000 34–35

Canada 1:15 000 000 36–37

Alaska

United States – West 1:6 700 000 38–39

United States – Midwest and North-east 1:6 700 000 40–41

United States – South 1:6 700 000 42–43

Mexico, Central America and the West Indies 1:15 000 000 44–45

Jamaica, Guadeloupe, Martinique, Puerto Rico,

Virgin Islands, St Lucia and Barbados

South America – North 1:16 000 000 46–47

Trinidad and Tobago

South America – South 1:16 000 000 48

Index to World Maps 49–57

Published in 2024 by Philip's,
a division of Octopus Publishing Group Limited
(www.octopusbooks.co.uk)
Carmelite House, 50 Victoria Embankment,
London EC4Y 0DZ
An Hachette UK Company (www.hachette.co.uk)

in association with
Hachette Aotearoa New Zealand
(an imprint of Hachette New Zealand Pty Limited)
Level 2, 23 O'Connell Street, Auckland, New Zealand
www.hachette.co.nz

Cartography by Philip's

ISBN 978-1-86971-580-9

A catalogue record for this book is available from the National Library of New Zealand.

Printed in Malaysia

Details of other Philip's titles and services can be found on our website at: www.philips-maps.co.uk

ACKNOWLEDGEMENTS
Cover image: LWM/NASA/LANDSAT / Alamy Stock Photo

World Statistics: Countries

This alphabetical list includes the principal countries and territories of the world. If a territory is not completely independent, the country it is associated with is named. The area figures give the total area of land, inland water and ice. The population figures are 2024 estimates where available. The annual income is the real Gross Domestic Product per capita (PPP) in US dollars. The figures are the latest available.

untry/Territory	Area km² Thousands	Area miles² Thousands	Population Thousands	Capital	Annual Income US $
ghanistan	652	252	40,122	Kabul	1,500
bania	28.7	11.1	3,107	Tirana	15,500
geria	2,382	920	47,022	Algiers	11,200
merican Samoa (US)	0.20	0.08	44	Pago Pago	11,200
ndorra	0.47	0.18	85	Andorra La Vella	49,900
ngola	1,247	481	37,202	Luanda	5,900
nguilla (UK)	0.10	0.04	19	The Valley	12,200
ntigua & Barbuda	0.44	0.17	103	St John's	22,300
gentina	2,780	1,074	46,994	Buenos Aires	22,500
menia	29.8	11.5	2,977	Yerevan	16,100
ruba (Netherlands)	0.19	0.07	125	Oranjestad	41,300
ustralia	7,741	2,989	26,769	Canberra	51,100
ustria	83.9	32.4	8,968	Vienna	55,900
zerbaijan	86.6	33.4	10,650	Baku	15,100
zores (Portugal)	2.2	0.86	246	Ponta Delgada	15,200
ahamas, The	13.9	5.4	411	Nassau	34,700
ahrain	0.69	0.27	1,567	Manama	51,900
angladesh	144	55.6	168,697	Dhaka	6,300
arbados	0.43	0.17	304	Bridgetown	15,400
elarus	208	80.2	9,501	Minsk	19,100
elgium	30.5	11.8	11,978	Brussels	53,300
elize	23.0	8.9	416	Belmopan	9,500
enin	113	43.5	14,697	Porto-Novo	3,400
ermuda (UK)	0.05	0.02	73	Hamilton	81,200
hutan	47.0	18.1	885	Thimphu	11,600
olivia	1,099	424	12,312	La Paz/Sucre	8,200
osnia-Herzegovina	51.2	19.8	3,799	Sarajevo	16,700
otswana	582	225	2,451	Gaborone	15,500
azil	8,514	3,287	220,052	Brasília	15,100
unei	5.8	2.2	492	Bandar Seri Begawan	58,700
ulgaria	111	42.8	6,783	Sofia	27,000
urkina Faso	274	106	23,042	Ouagadougou	2,200
urundi	27.8	10.7	13,590	Gitega	700
abo Verde	4.0	1.6	611	Praia	7,400
ambodia	181	69.9	17,064	Phnom Penh	4,500
ameroon	475	184	30,966	Yaoundé	3,700
anada	9,971	3,850	38,795	Ottawa	49,000
anary Is. (Spain)	7.2	2.8	2,105	Las Palmas/Santa Cruz	19,900
ayman Is. (UK)	0.26	0.10	67	George Town	71,400
entral African Republic	623	241	5,651	Bangui	800
had	1,284	496	19,094	Ndjaména	1,400
hile	757	292	18,665	Santiago	25,900
hina	9,597	3,705	1,416,043	Beijing	18,200
olombia	1,139	440	49,588	Bogotá	15,600
omoros	2.2	0.86	900	Moroni	3,200
ongo	342	132	6,098	Brazzaville	3,700
ongo (Dem. Rep. of the)	2,345	905	115,403	Kinshasa	1,100
ook Is. (NZ)	0.24	0.09	8	Avarua	15,600
osta Rica	51.1	19.7	5,266	San José	22,100
ôte d'Ivoire (Ivory Coast)	322	125	29,982	Yamoussoukro	5,500
roatia	56.5	21.8	4,150	Zagreb	34,300
uba	111	42.8	10,966	Havana	12,300
uraçao (Netherlands)	0.44	0.17	153	Willemstad	23,100
yprus	9.3	3.6	1,321	Nicosia	45,000
zechia	78.9	30.5	10,838	Prague	41,100
enmark	43.1	16.6	5,973	Copenhagen	59,900
jibouti	23.2	9.0	995	Djibouti	5,000
ominica	0.75	0.29	75	Roseau	11,500
ominican Republic	48.5	18.7	10,816	Santo Domingo	19,300
uador	284	109	18,310	Quito	10,900
ypt	1,001	387	111,247	Cairo	12,800
Salvador	21.0	8.1	6,629	San Salvador	9,400
quatorial Guinea	28.1	10.8	1,796	Malabo	14,900
itrea	118	45.4	6,344	Asmara	1,600
tonia	45.1	17.4	1,194	Tallinn	37,700
watini (Swaziland)	17.4	6.7	1,138	Mbabane/Lobamba	9,100
hiopia	1,104	426	118,550	Addis Ababa	2,400
lkland Is. (UK)	12.2	4.7	3	Stanley	70,800
roe Is. (Denmark)	1.4	0.54	53	Tórshavn	40,000
i	18.3	7.1	952	Suva	12,400
nland	338	131	5,626	Helsinki	49,400
ance	552	213	68,375	Paris	45,900
ench Guiana (France)	90.0	34.7	250	Cayenne	8,300
ench Polynesia (France)	4.0	1.5	304	Papeete	18,600
abon	268	103	2,455	Libreville	13,900
ambia, The	11.3	4.4	2,523	Banjul	2,100
eorgia	69.7	26.9	4,901	Tbilisi	17,100
ermany	357	138	84,119	Berlin	54,000
hana	239	92.1	34,589	Accra	5,500
braltar (UK)	0.006	0.002	30	Gibraltar Town	61,700
eece	132	50.9	10,461	Athens	31,700
eenland (Denmark)	2,176	840	58	Nuuk	41,800
enada	0.34	0.13	115	St George's	14,500
uadeloupe (France)	1.7	0.66	402	Basse-Terre	7,900
uam (US)	0.55	0.21	170	Hagatna	35,600
uatemala	109	42.0	18,255	Guatemala City	9,200
uinea	246	94.9	13,986	Conakry	2,700
uinea-Bissau	36.1	13.9	2,132	Bissau	1,900
uyana	215	83.0	794	Georgetown	35,600
aiti	27.8	10.7	11,754	Port-au-Prince	2,800
onduras	112	43.3	9,529	Tegucigalpa	5,700
ungary	93.0	35.9	9,856	Budapest	35,400
eland	103	39.8	364	Reykjavik	55,600
dia	3,287	1,269	1,409,128	New Delhi	7,100
donesia	1,905	735	281,562	Jakarta/Nusantara	12,400
an	1,648	636	88,387	Tehran	15,500
aq	438	169	42,083	Baghdad	9,200
eland	70.3	27.1	5,233	Dublin	112,400
rael	20.6	8.0	9,043	Jerusalem	44,400
aly	301	116	60,965	Rome	44,300
maica	11.0	4.2	2,824	Kingston	10,100
pan	378	146	123,202	Tokyo	41,600
rdan	89.3	34.5	11,174	Amman	9,500
azakhstan	2,725	1,052	20,260	Astana	26,100
enya	580	224	58,246	Nairobi	4,900
ribati	0.73	0.28	117	Tarawa	2,000
orea, North	121	46.5	26,299	Pyŏngyang	1,700
orea, South	99.3	38.3	52,082	Seoul	45,600
osovo	10.9	4.2	1,977	Pristina	12,700
uwait	17.8	6.9	3,138	Kuwait City	49,400
rgyzstan	200	77.2	6,172	Bishkek	5,100
os	237	91.4	7,954	Vientiane	7,900

Country/Territory	Area km² Thousands	Area miles² Thousands	Population Thousands	Capital	Annual Income US $
Latvia	64.6	24.9	1,801	Riga	33,000
Lebanon	10.4	4.0	5,364	Beirut	13,000
Lesotho	30.4	11.7	2,228	Maseru	2,200
Liberia	111	43.0	5,437	Monrovia	1,500
Libya	1,760	679	7,361	Tripoli	19,800
Liechtenstein	0.16	0.06	40	Vaduz	139,100
Lithuania	65.2	25.2	2,628	Vilnius	40,000
Luxembourg	2.6	1.0	671	Luxembourg	117,700
Macedonia, North	25.7	9.9	2,136	Skopje	17,100
Madagascar	587	227	29,453	Antananarivo	1,500
Madeira (Portugal)	0.78	0.30	289	Funchal	25,800
Malawi	118	45.7	21,763	Lilongwe	1,500
Malaysia	330	127	34,565	Kuala Lumpur/Putrajaya	28,400
Maldives	0.30	0.12	389	Malé	21,300
Mali	1,240	479	21,991	Bamako	2,100
Malta	0.32	0.12	470	Valletta	48,600
Marshall Is.	0.18	0.07	82	Majuro	6,000
Martinique (France)	1.1	0.43	386	Fort-de-France	14,400
Mauritania	1,026	396	4,328	Nouakchott	5,300
Mauritius	2.0	0.79	1,311	Port Louis	22,800
Mayotte (France)	0.37	0.14	213	Mamoudzou	4,900
Mexico	1,958	756	130,740	Mexico City	20,300
Micronesia, Fed. States of	0.70	0.27	100	Palikir	3,300
Moldova	33.9	13.1	3,600	Chisinau	13,300
Monaco	0.002	0.0008	32	Monaco	115,700
Mongolia	1,567	605	3,282	Ulan Bator	12,100
Montenegro	14.0	5.4	600	Podgorica	22,100
Montserrat (UK)	0.10	0.39	5	Brades	34,000
Morocco	447	172	37,388	Rabat	8,100
Mozambique	802	309	33,351	Maputo	1,300
Myanmar (Burma)	677	261	57,527	Naypyidaw	4,200
Namibia	824	318	2,804	Windhoek	9,800
Nauru	0.02	0.008	10	Yaren	11,000
Nepal	147	56.8	31,122	Katmandu	4,000
Netherlands	41.5	16.0	17,772	Amsterdam/The Hague	59,200
New Caledonia (France)	18.6	7.2	304	Nouméa	35,700
New Zealand	271	104	5,161	Wellington	45,200
Nicaragua	130	50.2	6,244	Managua	5,800
Niger	1,267	489	26,343	Niamey	1,300
Nigeria	924	357	236,747	Abuja	5,000
Northern Mariana Is. (US)	0.46	0.18	51	Saipan	24,500
Norway	324	125	5,510	Oslo	67,500
Oman	310	119	3,902	Muscat	35,300
Pakistan	796	307	252,364	Islamabad	5,400
Palau	0.46	0.18	22	Ngerulmud	14,100
Panama	75.5	29.2	4,470	Panamá City	33,300
Papua New Guinea	463	179	10,046	Port Moresby	3,800
Paraguay	407	157	7,523	Asunción	13,500
Peru	1,285	496	32,600	Lima	12,700
Philippines	300	116	118,277	Manila	8,600
Poland	323	125	38,746	Warsaw	37,700
Portugal	88.8	34.3	10,207	Lisbon	35,800
Puerto Rico (US)	8.9	3.4	3,019	San Juan	34,300
Qatar	11.0	4.2	2,552	Doha	96,600
Réunion (France)	2.5	0.97	846	St-Denis	6,200
Romania	238	92.0	18,148	Bucharest	32,500
Russia	17,075	6,593	140,821	Moscow	27,500
Rwanda	26.3	10.2	13,623	Kigali	2,400
St Kitts & Nevis	0.26	0.10	55	Basseterre	28,800
St Lucia	0.54	0.21	168	Castries	15,100
St Vincent & Grenadines	0.39	0.15	101	Kingstown	14,600
Samoa	2.8	1.1	209	Apia	5,200
San Marino	0.06	0.02	35	San Marino	61,600
São Tomé & Príncipe	0.96	0.37	224	São Tomé	3,400
Saudi Arabia	2,150	830	36,544	Riyadh	50,200
Senegal	197	76.0	18,848	Dakar	3,600
Serbia	77.5	29.9	6,652	Belgrade	20,900
Seychelles	0.46	0.18	98	Victoria	25,200
Sierra Leone	71.7	27.7	9,121	Freetown	1,600
Singapore	0.68	0.26	6,028	Singapore City	108,000
Slovakia	49.0	18.9	5,564	Bratislava	33,200
Slovenia	20.3	7.8	2,098	Ljubljana	41,000
Solomon Is.	28.9	11.2	727	Honiara	2,200
Somalia	638	246	13,017	Mogadishu	1,400
South Africa	1,221	471	60,443	Cape Town/Pretoria	13,500
Spain	498	192	47,280	Madrid	40,200
Sri Lanka	65.6	25.3	21,983	Colombo	12,200
Sudan	1,886	728	50,467	Khartoum	3,600
Sudan, South	620	239	12,704	Juba	1,600
Suriname	163	63.0	647	Paramaribo	15,000
Sweden	450	174	10,590	Stockholm	55,300
Switzerland	41.3	15.9	8,861	Bern	72,300
Syria	185	71.5	23,865	Damascus	2,900
Taiwan	36.0	13.9	23,595	Taipei	47,800
Tajikistan	143	55.3	10,394	Dushanbe	4,100
Tanzania	945	365	67,462	Dodoma	2,600
Thailand	513	198	69,921	Bangkok	17,500
Timor-Leste (East Timor)	14.9	5.7	1,507	Dili	3,900
Togo	56.8	21.9	8,918	Lomé	2,200
Tonga	0.65	0.25	105	Nuku'alofa	6,100
Trinidad & Tobago	5.1	2.0	1,409	Port of Spain	23,300
Tunisia	164	63.2	12,049	Tunis	10,600
Turkey	775	299	84,120	Ankara	33,100
Turkmenistan	488	188	5,744	Ashkhabad	14,700
Turks & Caicos Is. (UK)	0.43	0.17	60	Cockburn Town	20,700
Tuvalu	0.03	0.01	12	Funafuti	4,600
Uganda	241	93.1	49,283	Kampala	2,300
Ukraine	604	233	35,662	Kyiv	10,700
United Arab Emirates	83.6	32.3	10,032	Abu Dhabi	74,900
United Kingdom	242	93.4	68,459	London	47,600
United States of America	9,629	3,718	341,963	Washington, DC	64,600
Uruguay	175	67.6	3,425	Montevideo	24,400
Uzbekistan	447	173	36,521	Tashkent	8,100
Vanuatu	12.2	4.7	318	Port-Vila	2,800
Vatican City	0.0004	0.0002	1	Vatican City	-
Venezuela	912	352	31,250	Caracas	7,704
Vietnam	332	128	105,759	Hanoi	11,400
Virgin Is. (UK)	0.15	0.06	40	Road Town	34,200
Virgin Is. (US)	0.35	0.13	104	Charlotte Amalie	37,000
Yemen	528	204	32,140	Sana'	2,500
Zambia	753	291	20,799	Lusaka	3,400
Zimbabwe	391	151	17,150	Harare	2,200

World Statistics: Physical Dimensions

Each topic list is divided into continents and within a continent the items are listed in order of size. The bottom part of many of the lists is selective in order to give examples from as many different countries as possible. The order of the continents is the same as in the atlas, beginning with Europe and ending with South America. The figures are rounded as appropriate.

World, Continents, Oceans

	km²	miles²	%
The World	509,450,000	196,672,000	–
Land	149,450,000	57,688,000	29.3
Water	360,000,000	138,984,000	70.7
Asia	44,500,000	17,177,000	29.8
Africa	30,302,000	11,697,000	20.3
North America	24,241,000	9,357,000	16.2
South America	17,793,000	6,868,000	11.9
Antarctica	14,100,000	5,443,000	9.4
Europe	9,957,000	3,843,000	6.7
Australia and Oceania	8,557,000	3,303,000	5.7
Pacific Ocean	155,557,000	60,061,000	46.4
Atlantic Ocean	76,762,000	29,638,000	22.9
Indian Ocean	68,556,000	26,470,000	20.4
Southern Ocean	20,327,000	7,848,000	6.1
Arctic Ocean	14,056,000	5,427,000	4.2

Ocean Depths

Atlantic Ocean	m	ft
Puerto Rico (Milwaukee) Deep	8,605	28,232
Cayman Trench	7,680	25,197
Gulf of Mexico	5,203	17,070
Mediterranean Sea	5,121	16,801
Black Sea	2,211	7,254
North Sea	660	2,165

Indian Ocean	m	ft
Java Trench	7,450	24,442
Red Sea	2,635	8,454

Pacific Ocean	m	ft
Mariana Trench	11,022	36,161
Tonga Trench	10,882	35,702
Japan Trench	10,554	34,626
Kuril Trench	10,542	34,587

Arctic Ocean	m	ft
Molloy Deep	5,608	18,399

Southern Ocean	m	ft
South Sandwich Trench	7,235	23,737

Mountains

Europe		m	ft
Elbrus	*Russia*	5,642	18,510
Dykh-Tau	*Russia*	5,205	17,076
Shkhara	*Russia/Georgia*	5,201	17,064
Koshtan-Tau	*Russia*	5,152	16,903
Kazbek	*Russia/Georgia*	5,047	16,558
Pushkin	*Russia/Georgia*	5,033	16,512
Katyn-Tau	*Russia/Georgia*	4,979	16,335
Shota Rustaveli	*Russia/Georgia*	4,860	15,945
Mont Blanc	*France/Italy*	4,808	15,774
Monte Rosa	*Italy/Switzerland*	4,634	15,203
Dom	*Switzerland*	4,545	14,911
Liskamm	*Switzerland*	4,527	14,852
Weisshorn	*Switzerland*	4,505	14,780
Taschorn	*Switzerland*	4,490	14,730
Matterhorn/Cervino	*Italy/Switzerland*	4,478	14,691
Grossglockner	*Austria*	3,797	12,457
Mulhacén	*Spain*	3,478	11,411
Zugspitze	*Germany*	2,962	9,718
Olympus	*Greece*	2,917	9,570
Galdhøpiggen	*Norway*	2,469	8,100
Ben Nevis	*UK*	1,345	4,411

Asia		m	ft
Everest	*China/Nepal*	8,849	29,032
K2 (Godwin Austen)	*China/Kashmir*	8,611	28,251
Kanchenjunga	*India/Nepal*	8,598	28,208
Lhotse	*China/Nepal*	8,516	27,939
Makalu	*China/Nepal*	8,481	27,824
Cho Oyu	*China/Nepal*	8,201	26,906
Dhaulagiri	*Nepal*	8,167	26,795
Manaslu	*Nepal*	8,156	26,758
Nanga Parbat	*Kashmir*	8,126	26,660
Annapurna	*Nepal*	8,078	26,502
Gasherbrum	*China/Kashmir*	8,068	26,469
Broad Peak	*China/Kashmir*	8,051	26,414
Xixabangma	*China*	8,012	26,286
Kangbachen	*Nepal*	7,858	25,781
Trivor	*Pakistan*	7,720	25,328
Pik Imeni Ismail Samani	*Tajikistan*	7,495	24,590
Demavend	*Iran*	5,604	18,386
Ararat	*Turkey*	5,165	16,945
Gunong Kinabalu	*Malaysia (Borneo)*	4,101	13,455
Fuji-San	*Japan*	3,776	12,388

Africa		m	ft
Kilimanjaro	*Tanzania*	5,895	19,340
Mt Kenya	*Kenya*	5,199	17,057
Ruwenzori (Margherita)	*Ug./Congo (D.R.)*	5,109	16,762
Meru	*Tanzania*	4,565	14,977
Ras Dashen	*Ethiopia*	4,553	14,937
Karisimbi	*Rwanda/Congo (D.R.)*	4,507	14,787
Mt Elgon	*Kenya/Uganda*	4,321	14,176
Batu	*Ethiopia*	4,307	14,130
Toubkal	*Morocco*	4,165	13,665
Mt Cameroun	*Cameroon*	4,070	13,353

Oceania		m	ft
Puncak Jaya	*Indonesia*	4,884	16,024
Puncak Trikora	*Indonesia*	4,730	15,518
Puncak Mandala	*Indonesia*	4,702	15,427
Mt Wilhelm	*Papua New Guinea*	4,508	14,790
Mauna Kea	*USA (Hawai'i)*	4,205	13,796
Mauna Loa	*USA (Hawai'i)*	4,169	13,678
Aoraki Mt Cook	*New Zealand*	3,724	12,218
Mt Kosciuszko	*Australia*	2,228	7,310

North America		m	ft
Denali (Mt McKinley)	*USA (Alaska)*	6,190	20,310
Mt Logan	*Canada*	5,959	19,551
Pico de Orizaba	*Mexico*	5,610	18,405
Mt St Elias	*USA/Canada*	5,489	18,008
Popocatépetl	*Mexico*	5,452	17,887
Mt Foraker	*USA (Alaska)*	5,304	17,401
Iztaccihuatl	*Mexico*	5,286	17,342
Lucania	*Canada*	5,226	17,146
Mt Steele	*Canada*	5,073	16,644
Mt Bona	*USA (Alaska)*	5,005	16,420
Mt Whitney	*USA*	4,418	14,495
Tajumulco	*Guatemala*	4,220	13,845
Chirripó Grande	*Costa Rica*	3,837	12,589
Pico Duarte	*Dominican Rep.*	3,175	10,417

South America		m	ft
Aconcagua	*Argentina*	6,962	22,841
Bonete	*Argentina*	6,872	22,546
Ojos del Salado	*Argentina/Chile*	6,863	22,516
Pissis	*Argentina*	6,779	22,241
Mercedario	*Argentina/Chile*	6,770	22,211
Huascarán	*Peru*	6,768	22,204
Llullaillaco	*Argentina/Chile*	6,723	22,057
Nevado de Cachi	*Argentina*	6,720	22,047
Yerupaja	*Peru*	6,632	21,758
Sajama	*Bolivia*	6,520	21,391
Chimborazo	*Ecuador*	6,267	20,561
Pico Cristóbal Colón	*Colombia*	5,800	19,029
Pico Bolivar	*Venezuela*	5,007	16,427

Antarctica		m	ft
Vinson Massif		4,897	16,066
Mt Kirkpatrick		4,528	14,855

Rivers

Europe		km	miles
Volga	*Caspian Sea*	3,700	2,300
Danube	*Black Sea*	2,850	1,770
Ural	*Caspian Sea*	2,535	1,575
Dnieper	*Black Sea*	2,285	1,420
Kama	*Volga*	2,030	1,260
Don	*Black Sea*	1,990	1,240
Petchora	*Arctic Ocean*	1,790	1,110
Oka	*Volga*	1,480	920
Dniester	*Black Sea*	1,400	870
Vyatka	*Kama*	1,370	850
Rhine	*North Sea*	1,320	820
N. Dvina	*Arctic Ocean*	1,290	800
Elbe	*North Sea*	1,145	710

Asia		km	miles
Yangtse	*Pacific Ocean*	6,380	3,960
Yenisey–Angara	*Arctic Ocean*	5,550	3,445
Huang He	*Pacific Ocean*	5,464	3,395
Ob–Irtysh	*Arctic Ocean*	5,410	3,360
Mekong	*Pacific Ocean*	4,500	2,795
Amur	*Pacific Ocean*	4,442	2,760
Lena	*Arctic Ocean*	4,402	2,735
Irtysh	*Ob*	4,250	2,640
Yenisey	*Arctic Ocean*	4,090	2,540
Ob	*Arctic Ocean*	3,680	2,285
Indus	*Indian Ocean*	3,100	1,925
Brahmaputra	*Indian Ocean*	2,900	1,800
Syrdarya	*Aralkum Desert*	2,860	1,775
Salween	*Indian Ocean*	2,800	1,740
Euphrates	*Indian Ocean*	2,700	1,675
Amudarya	*Aralkum Desert*	2,540	1,575

Africa		km	miles
Nile	*Mediterranean*	6,695	4,160
Congo	*Atlantic Ocean*	4,670	2,900
Niger	*Atlantic Ocean*	4,180	2,595
Zambezi	*Indian Ocean*	3,540	2,200
Oubangi/Uele	*Congo (D.R.)*	2,250	1,400
Kasai	*Congo (D.R.)*	1,950	1,210
Shaballe	*Indian Ocean*	1,930	1,200
Orange	*Atlantic Ocean*	1,860	1,155
Cubango	*Okavango Delta*	1,800	1,120
Limpopo	*Indian Ocean*	1,770	1,100
Senegal	*Atlantic Ocean*	1,640	1,020

Australia		km	miles
Murray–Darling	*Southern Ocean*	3,750	2,330
Darling	*Murray*	3,070	1,905
Murray	*Southern Ocean*	2,575	1,600
Murrumbidgee	*Murray*	1,690	1,050

North America		km	miles
Mississippi–Missouri	*Gulf of Mexico*	5,971	3,710
Mackenzie	*Arctic Ocean*	4,240	2,630
Missouri	*Mississippi*	4,088	2,540
Mississippi	*Gulf of Mexico*	3,782	2,350
Yukon	*Pacific Ocean*	3,185	1,980
Rio Grande	*Gulf of Mexico*	3,030	1,880
Arkansas	*Mississippi*	2,340	1,450
Colorado	*Pacific Ocean*	2,330	1,445
Red	*Mississippi*	2,040	1,270
Columbia	*Pacific Ocean*	1,950	1,210
Saskatchewan	*Lake Winnipeg*	1,940	1,205

South America		km	miles
Amazon	*Atlantic Ocean*	6,450	4,010
Paraná–Plate	*Atlantic Ocean*	4,500	2,800
Purus	*Amazon*	3,350	2,080
Madeira	*Amazon*	3,200	1,990
São Francisco	*Atlantic Ocean*	2,900	1,800
Paraná	*Plate*	2,800	1,740
Tocantins	*Atlantic Ocean*	2,750	1,710
Orinoco	*Atlantic Ocean*	2,740	1,700
Paraguay	*Paraná*	2,550	1,580
Pilcomayo	*Paraná*	2,500	1,550
Araguaia	*Tocantins*	2,250	1,400

Lakes

Europe		km²	miles²
Lake Ladoga	*Russia*	17,700	6,800
Lake Onega	*Russia*	9,700	3,700
Saimaa system	*Finland*	8,000	3,100
Vänern	*Sweden*	5,500	2,100

Asia		km²	miles²
Caspian Sea	*Asia*	371,000	143,000
Lake Baikal	*Russia*	30,500	11,780
Tonlé Sap	*Cambodia*	20,000	7,700
Lake Balqash	*Kazakhstan*	18,500	7,100
Aral Sea	*Kazakhstan/Uzbekistan*	17,160	6,625

Africa		km²	miles²
Lake Victoria	*East Africa*	68,000	26,300
Lake Tanganyika	*Central Africa*	33,000	13,000
Lake Malawi/Nyasa	*East Africa*	29,600	11,430
Lake Chad	*Central Africa*	25,000	9,700
Lake Turkana	*Ethiopia/Kenya*	8,500	3,290
Lake Volta	*Ghana*	8,480	3,270

Australia		km²	miles²
Lake Eyre	*Australia*	8,900	3,400
Lake Torrens	*Australia*	5,800	2,200
Lake Gairdner	*Australia*	4,800	1,900

North America		km²	miles²
Lake Superior	*Canada/USA*	82,350	31,800
Lake Huron	*Canada/USA*	59,600	23,010
Lake Michigan	*USA*	58,000	22,400
Great Bear Lake	*Canada*	31,800	12,280
Great Slave Lake	*Canada*	28,500	11,000
Lake Erie	*Canada/USA*	25,700	9,900
Lake Winnipeg	*Canada*	24,400	9,400
Lake Ontario	*Canada/USA*	19,500	7,500
Lake Nicaragua	*Nicaragua*	8,200	3,200

South America		km²	miles²
Lake Titicaca	*Bolivia/Peru*	8,300	3,200
Lake Poopo	*Bolivia*	2,800	1,100

Islands

Europe		km²	miles²
Great Britain	*UK*	229,880	88,700
Iceland	*Atlantic Ocean*	103,000	39,800
Ireland	*Ireland/UK*	84,400	32,600
Novaya Zemlya (N.)	*Russia*	48,200	18,600
Sicily	*Italy*	25,500	9,800

Asia		km²	miles²
Borneo	*South-east Asia*	744,360	287,400
Sumatra	*Indonesia*	473,600	182,860
Honshu	*Japan*	230,500	88,980
Celebes	*Indonesia*	189,000	73,000
Java	*Indonesia*	126,700	48,900
Luzon	*Philippines*	104,700	40,400
Hokkaido	*Japan*	78,400	30,300

Africa		km²	miles²
Madagascar	*Indian Ocean*	587,040	226,660
Socotra	*Indian Ocean*	3,600	1,400
Réunion	*Indian Ocean*	2,500	965

Oceania		km²	miles²
New Guinea	*Indonesia/Papua NG*	821,030	317,000
New Zealand (S.)	*Pacific Ocean*	150,500	58,100
New Zealand (N.)	*Pacific Ocean*	114,700	44,300
Tasmania	*Australia*	67,800	26,200
Hawai'i	*Pacific Ocean*	10,450	4,000

North America		km²	miles²
Greenland	*Atlantic Ocean*	2,175,600	839,800
Baffin Is.	*Canada*	508,000	196,100
Victoria Is.	*Canada*	212,200	81,900
Ellesmere Is.	*Canada*	212,000	81,800
Cuba	*Caribbean Sea*	110,860	42,800
Hispaniola	*Dominican Rep./Haiti*	76,200	29,400
Jamaica	*Caribbean Sea*	11,400	4,400
Puerto Rico	*Atlantic Ocean*	8,900	3,400

South America		km²	miles²
Tierra del Fuego	*Argentina/Chile*	47,000	18,100
Chiloé	*Chile*	8,480	3,275
Falkland Is. (E.)	*Atlantic Ocean*	6,800	2,600

NEW ZEALAND MAPS

JANUARY TEMPERATURE

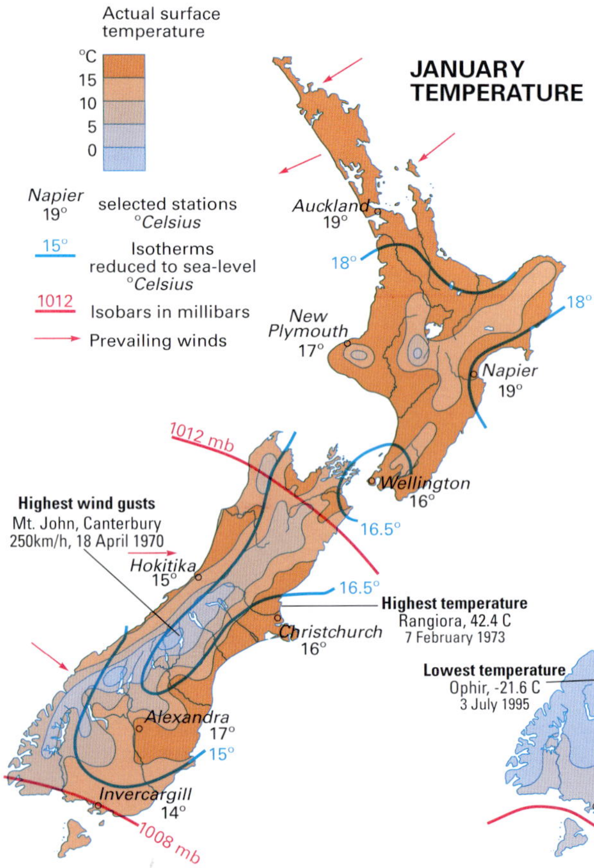

Actual surface temperature
°C
15
10
5
0

Napier 19° selected stations °Celsius
15° Isotherms reduced to sea-level °Celsius
1012 Isobars in millibars
Prevailing winds

Auckland 19°
18°
18°
New Plymouth 17°
Napier 19°
1012 mb
Wellington 16°
16.5°
16.5°
Highest wind gusts
Mt. John, Canterbury
250km/h, 18 April 1970
Hokitika 15°
Highest temperature
Rangiora, 42.4 C
7 February 1973
Christchurch 16°
Alexandra 17°
15°
Invercargill 14°
1008 mb

JULY TEMPERATURE

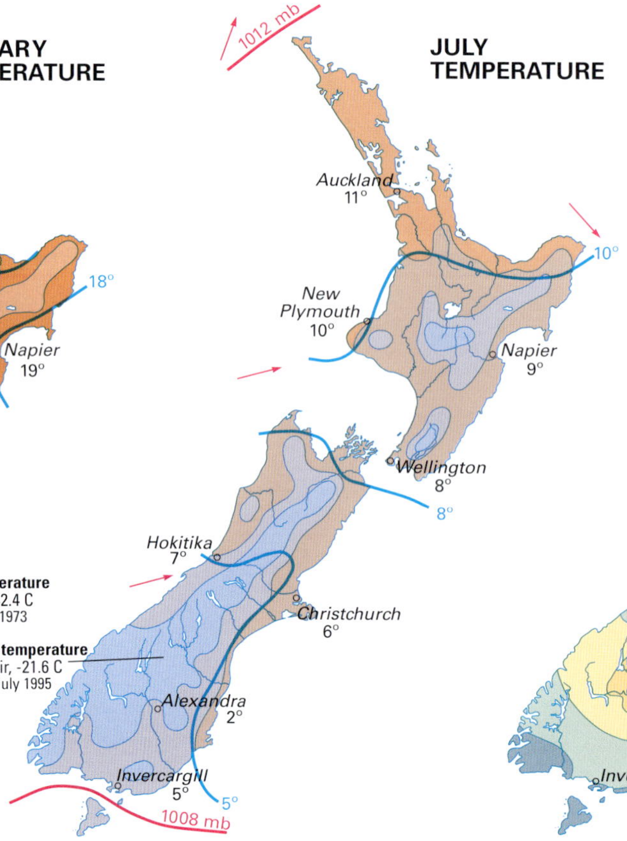

1012 mb
Auckland 11°
10°
New Plymouth 10°
Napier 9°
Wellington 8°
8°
Hokitika 7°
Lowest temperature
Ophir, -21.6 C
3 July 1995
Christchurch 6°
Alexandra 2°
Invercargill 5°
5°
1008 mb

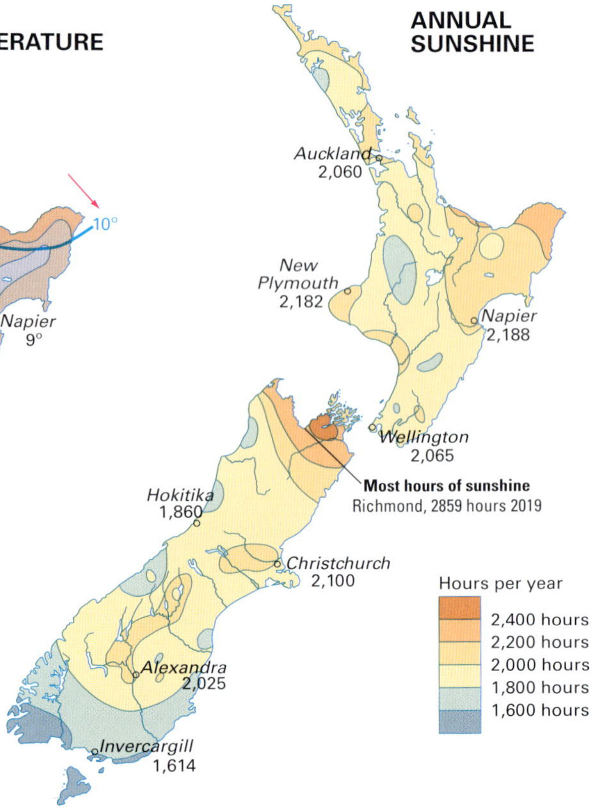

ANNUAL SUNSHINE

Auckland 2,060
New Plymouth 2,182
Napier 2,188
Wellington 2,065
Most hours of sunshine
Richmond, 2859 hours 2019
Hokitika 1,860
Christchurch 2,100
Alexandra 2,025
Invercargill 1,614

Hours per year
2,400 hours
2,200 hours
2,000 hours
1,800 hours
1,600 hours

ANNUAL RAINFALL

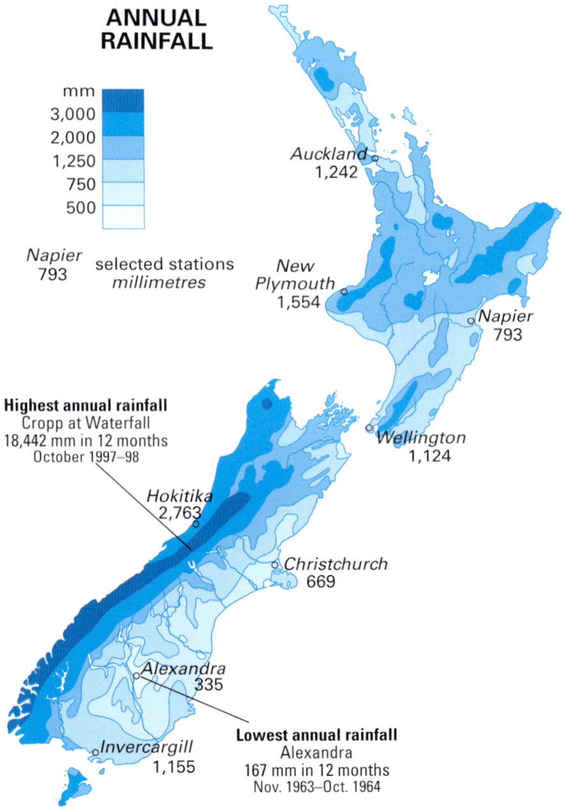

mm
3,000
2,000
1,250
750
500

Napier 793 selected stations millimetres

Auckland 1,242
New Plymouth 1,554
Napier 793
Highest annual rainfall
Cropp at Waterfall
18,442 mm in 12 months
October 1997–98
Wellington 1,124
Hokitika 2,763
Christchurch 669
Alexandra 335
Lowest annual rainfall
Alexandra
167 mm in 12 months
Nov. 1963–Oct. 1964
Invercargill 1,155

CLIMATE GRAPHS

WELLINGTON
°C
Temperature
30 20 10 0 -10 -20 -30 -40
Precipitation
1124mm
350 300 250 200 150 100 50
mm
J F M A M J J A S O N D

DUNEDIN
°C
Temperature
30 20 10 0 -10 -20 -30 -40
Precipitation
937mm
350 300 250 200 150 100 50
mm
J F M A M J J A S O N D

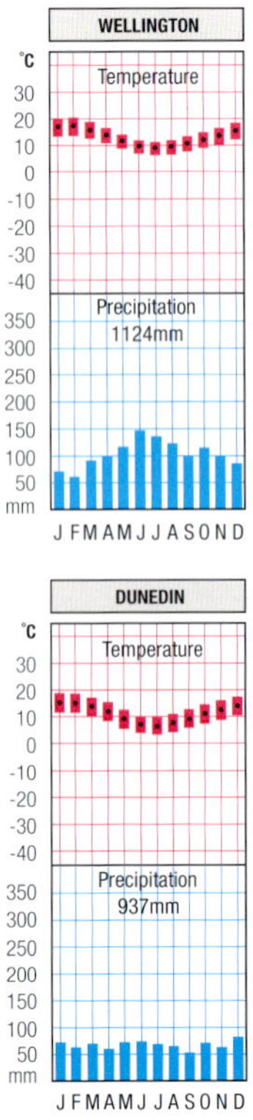

RAIN DAYS

Average number per year with 1.0 mm or more
200 days
150 days
100 days

Auckland 137
New Plymouth 138
Napier 91
Wellington 123
Hokitika 171
Christchurch 85
Alexandra 66
Invercargill 158

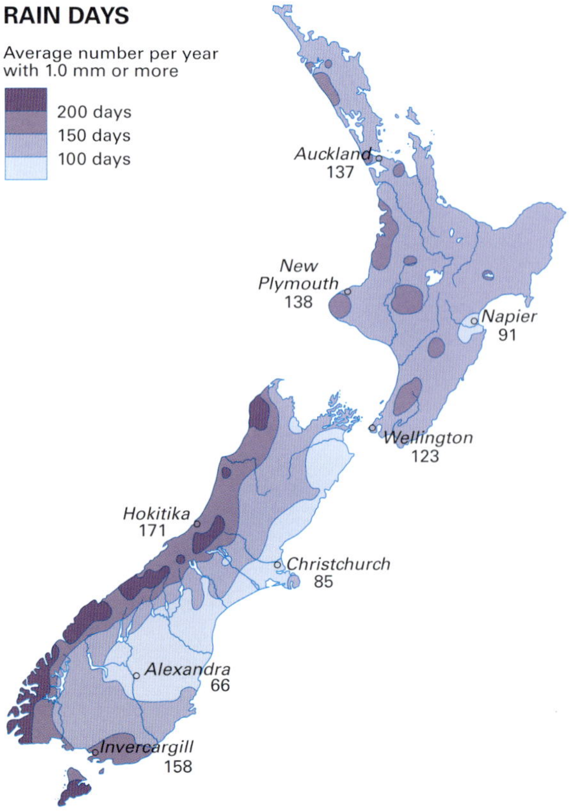

GEOLOGY

- Quaternary – sands, gravels, moraines
- Tertiary – sandstone, mudstone, siltstone
- Cretaceous – sandstone, mudstone, siltstone
- Jurassic and Triassic – greywacke, argillite
- Palaeozoic – mainly undifferentiated greywacke
- Pre-Cambrian – mainly undifferentiated greywacke
- Metamorphic and Plutonic – granitc, gneiss, schists
- Volcanic and Intrusive – basalts

NATURAL DISASTERS

From mid-19th century to present day

Date	Event	Consequences
1846 May	Landslide at Waihi, Lake Taupo	61 dead
1858 January	Floods in Hutt Valley	9 dead
1863 July	Snowstorm and floods in Otago	c. 100 dead
1886 June	Eruption of Mt. Tarawera	153 dead
1897 April	Tutaekuri flood	10 dead
1914 September	Eruption at Whakaari/White I.	11 dead
1929 June	Earthquake at Murchison	17 dead
1931 February	Earthquakes in Hawke's Bay	256 dead, 11,000 evacuated
1938 February	Flash flood at Kopuawhara	21 dead
1953 December	Lahar (volcanic mudflow) at Tangiwai	151 dead
1968 April	Cyclone Giselle	Over 50 dead
1968 May	Earthquake at Inangahua	3 dead, 300 evacuated
1988 March	Cyclone Bola	6 dead
2011 February	Christchurch earthquake	181 dead, many injured
2016 November	Kaikoura earthquake	2 dead
2019 December	Eruption at Whakaari/White I.	22 dead
2023 February	Cyclone Gabrielle	11 dead

CHRISTCHURCH EARTHQUAKE

- Tuesday 22 February 2011 at 12.51pm
- Magnitude 6.3 earthquake
- Epicentre in Lyttelton, 10 km south-east of central Christchurch
- Considered to be an aftershock of the 7.1 magnitude earthquake on 4 September 2010, epicentre in Darfield, 35 km west of Christchurch
- Brought down many buildings previously damaged in 2010 quake – one third of all buildings in Central Christchurch needed demolition

VOLCANOES

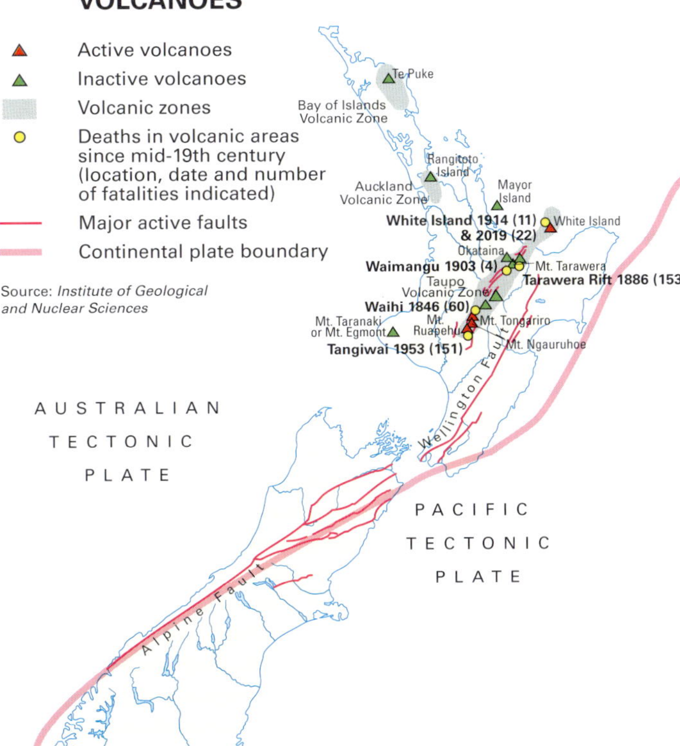

Source: *Institute of Geological and Nuclear Sciences*

AUSTRALIAN TECTONIC PLATE

PACIFIC TECTONIC PLATE

East Cape 23 February 1995 (7.0)
Hawke's Bay 3 February 1931 (7.8) 13 February 1931 (7.3)
Hawke's Bay 23 February 1863 (7.5)
Pahiatua 5 March 1934 (7.6)
Wairarapa 24 June 1942 (7.2)/2 August 1942 (7.0)
Wairarapa 23 January 1855 (8.1)
Cape Farewell 19 October 1868 (7.5)
Nelson 12 February 1893 (6.9)
Murchison 17 June 1929 (7.8)
Inangahua 24 May 1968 (7.1)
Wairau, Marlborough 16 October 1848 (7.5)
Kaikoura 14 November 2016 (7.8)
Arthur's Pass 9 March 1929 (7.1)
North Canterbury 1 September 1888 (7.3)
Darfield 4 September 2010 (7.1)
Christchurch 22 February 2011 (6.3) 13 June 2011 (5.9) 23 December 2011 (6.0)
Fiordland 22 August 2003 (7.1)
Wellington Fault
Alpine Fault

EARTHQUAKES

- Shallow (less than 40 km deep) earthquakes 1990–2011, over 5 on the Richter scale
- Deep (over 40 km deep) earthquakes 1990–2011, over 5 on the Richter scale
- Large shallow earthquakes since mid-19th century (location, date and magnitude are indicated)
- Major active faults
- Continental plate boundary

Source: *Institute of Geological and Nuclear Sciences*

POPULATION

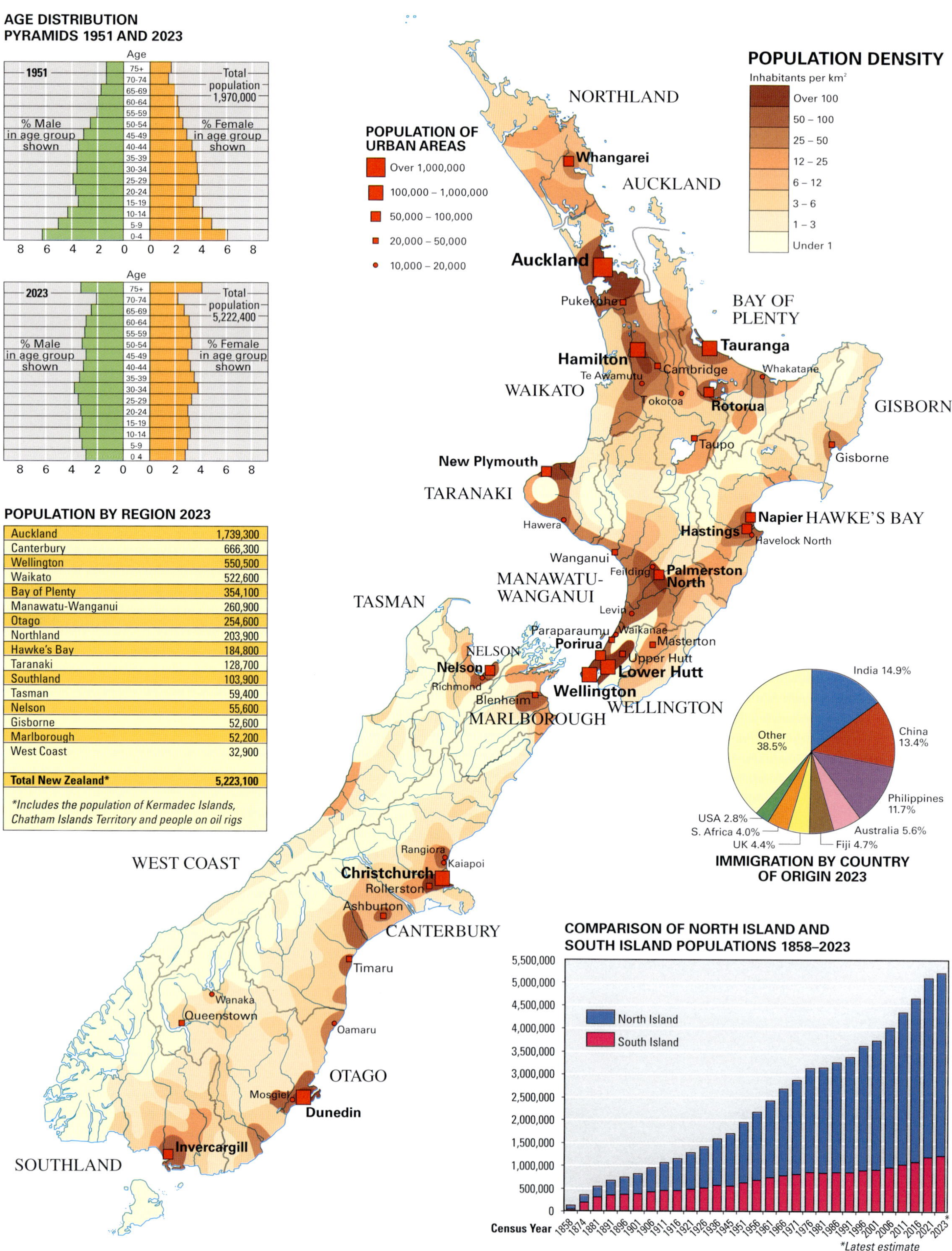

POPULATION BY REGION 2023

Auckland	1,739,300
Canterbury	666,300
Wellington	550,500
Waikato	522,600
Bay of Plenty	354,100
Manawatu-Wanganui	260,900
Otago	254,600
Northland	203,900
Hawke's Bay	184,800
Taranaki	128,700
Southland	103,900
Tasman	59,400
Nelson	55,600
Gisborne	52,600
Marlborough	52,200
West Coast	32,900
Total New Zealand*	**5,223,100**

**Includes the population of Kermadec Islands, Chatham Islands Territory and people on oil rigs*

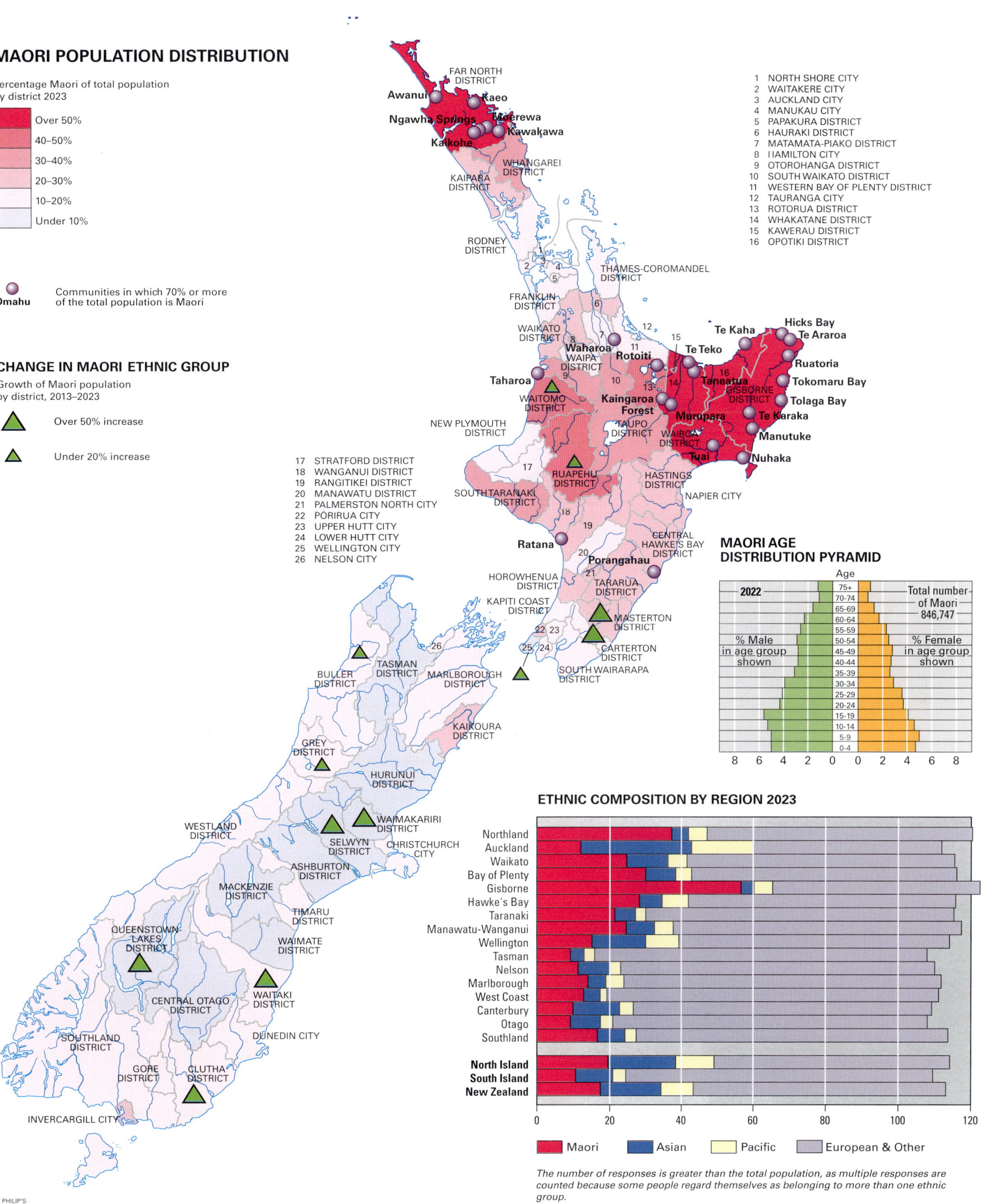

The number of responses is greater than the total population, as multiple responses are counted because some people regard themselves as belonging to more than one ethnic group.

LAND USE

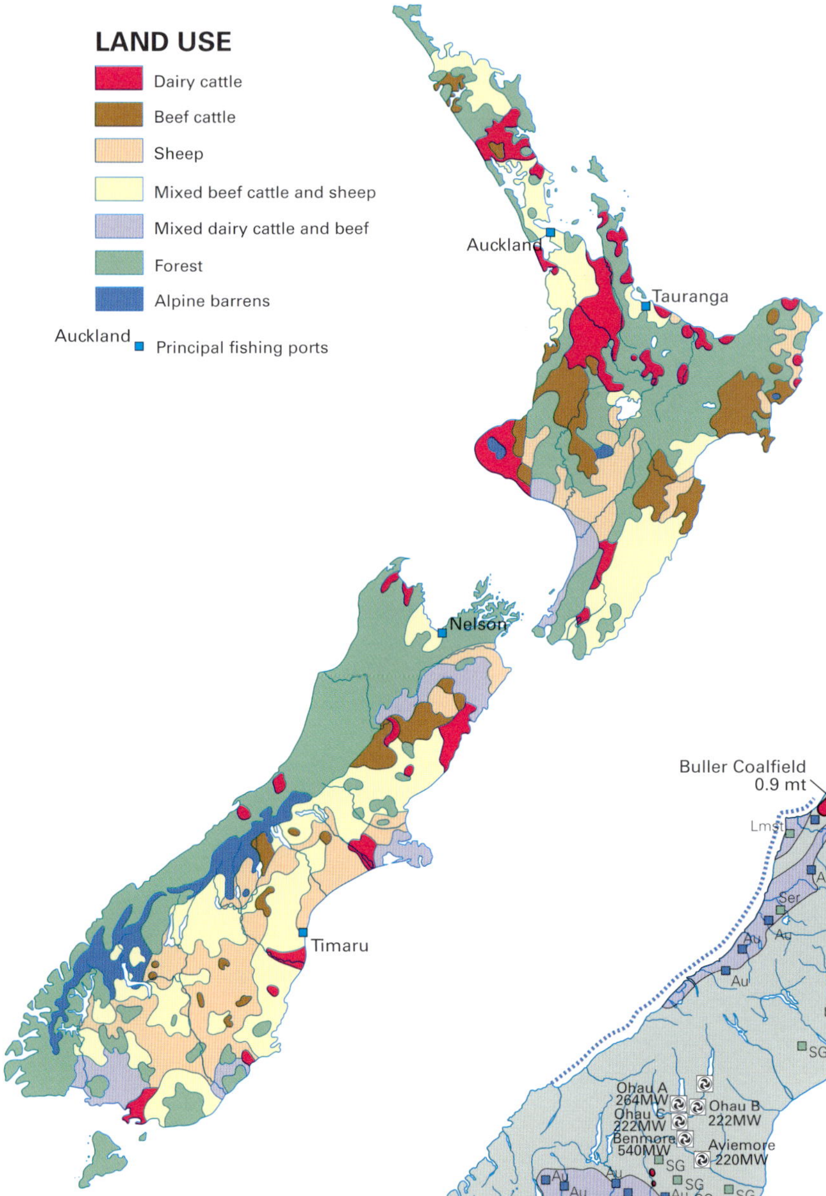

Dairy cattle
Beef cattle
Sheep
Mixed beef cattle and sheep
Mixed dairy cattle and beef
Forest
Alpine barrens
Auckland
Principal fishing ports
Auckland
Tauranga
Nelson
Timaru

MINERALS AND ENERGY RESOURCES

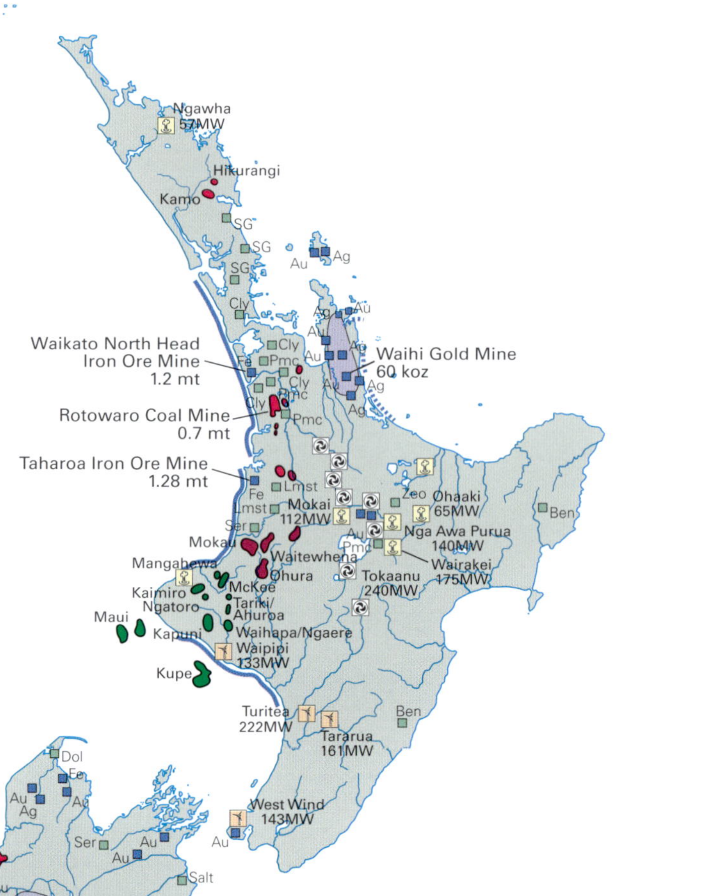

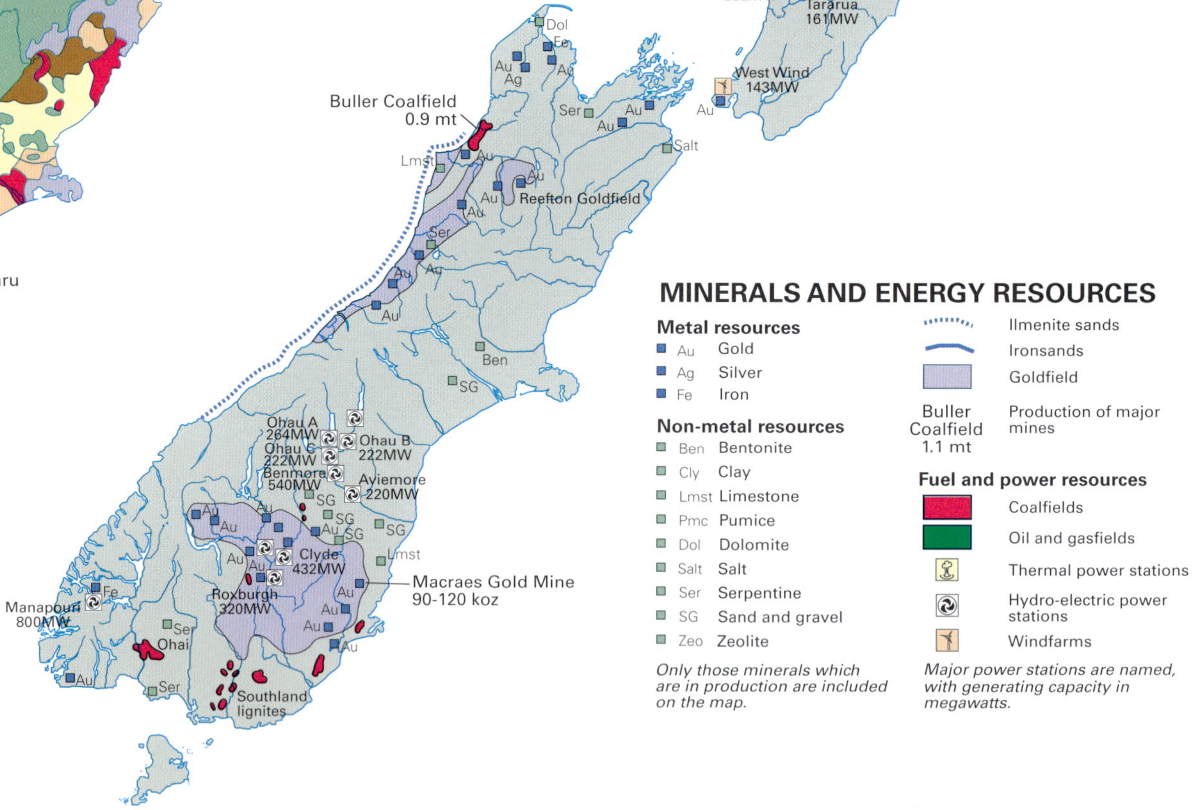

Ngawha 57MW
Hikurangi
Kamo
Waikato North Head Iron Ore Mine 1.2 mt
Waihi Gold Mine 60 koz
Rotowaro Coal Mine 0.7 mt
Taharoa Iron Ore Mine 1.28 mt
Mokai 112MW
Ohaaki 65MW
Nga Awa Purua 140MW
Wairakei 175MW
Tokaanu 240MW
Mokau
Waitewhena
Ohura
Mangahewa
McKee
Kaimiro
Ngatoro
Tariki/Ahuroa
Maui
Kapuni
Waihapa/Ngaere
Waipipi 133MW
Kupe
Turitea 222MW
Tararua 161MW
West Wind 143MW
Buller Coalfield 0.9 mt
Reefton Goldfield
Ohau A 264MW
Ohau B 222MW
Ohau C 222MW
Benmore 540MW
Aviemore 220MW
Clyde 432MW
Roxburgh 320MW
Macraes Gold Mine 90-120 koz
Manapouri 800MW
Ohai
Southland lignites
Metal resources
Au Gold
Ag Silver
Fe Iron
Non-metal resources
Ben Bentonite
Cly Clay
Lmst Limestone
Pmc Pumice
Dol Dolomite
Salt Salt
Ser Serpentine
SG Sand and gravel
Zeo Zeolite
Only those minerals which are in production are included on the map.
Ilmenite sands
Ironsands
Goldfield
Buller Coalfield 1.1 mt
Production of major mines
Fuel and power resources
Coalfields
Oil and gasfields
Thermal power stations
Hydro-electric power stations
Windfarms
Major power stations are named, with generating capacity in megawatts.

SEAFOOD EXPORTS

Oysters 1.1%
Other Molluscs 2.3%
Squid 6.7%
Mussels 16.0%
Fin Fish 50.2%
Other Crustacea 4.4%
Rock Lobster 17.6%
Other Fish 1.7%

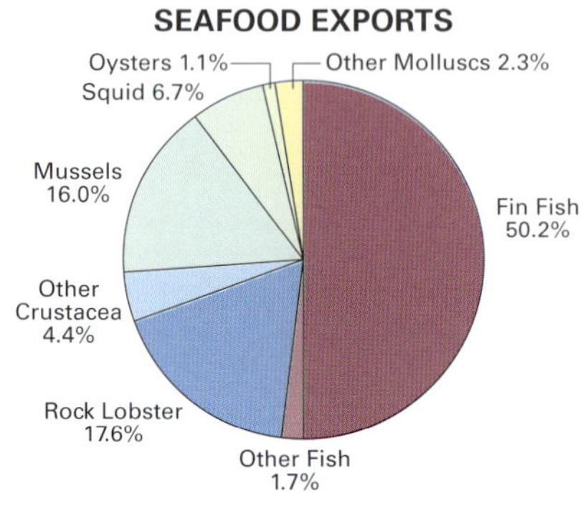

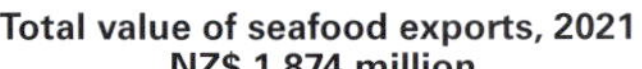

Total value of seafood exports, 2021
NZ$ 1,874 million

PRIMARY ENERGY PRODUCTION

Coal 5.1%
Wind 1.2%
Biomass & Solar 6.2%
Oil 35.1%
Hydro-electric 11.2%
Gas 16.9%
Geothermal 24.3%

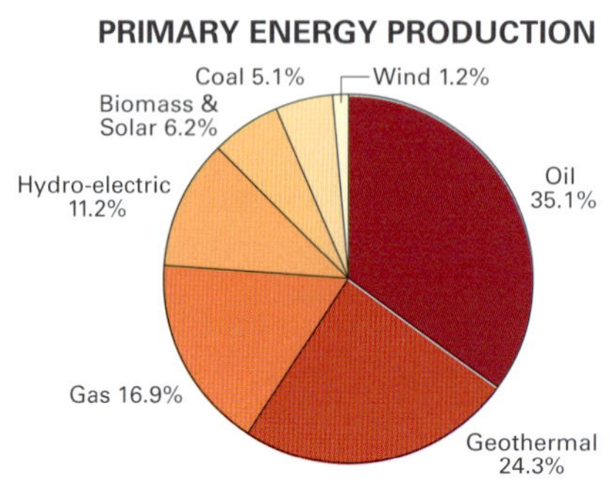

Total primary energy production, 2022
844.9 petajoules

PRIMARY ENERGY USE

Energy used (petajoules)
225
200
175
150
125
100
75
50
25
0
Transport
Industrial
Residential
Commercial
Agriculture

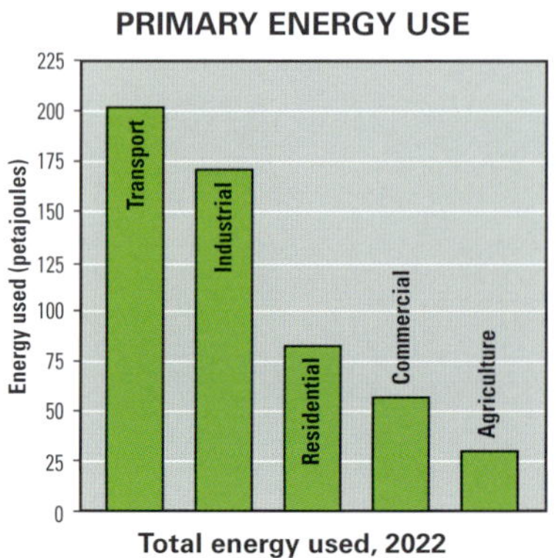

Total energy used, 2022
541.65 petajoules

TOURISM – ARRIVALS

Arrivals by overseas visitors, 2023

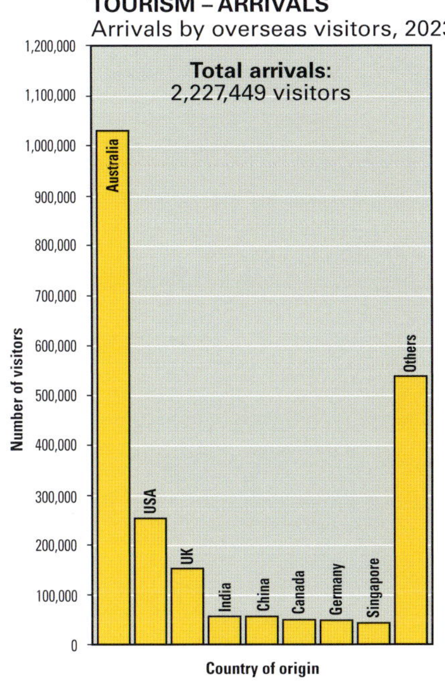

TOURISM – EXPENDITURE

Expenditure by overseas visitors, NZ$ million, 2019

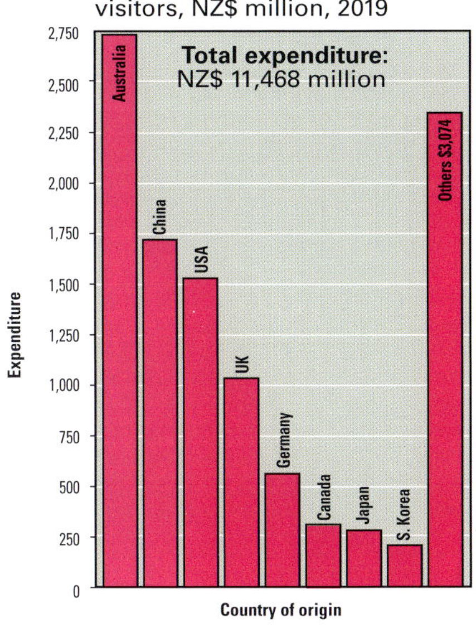

EMPLOYMENT BY REGION

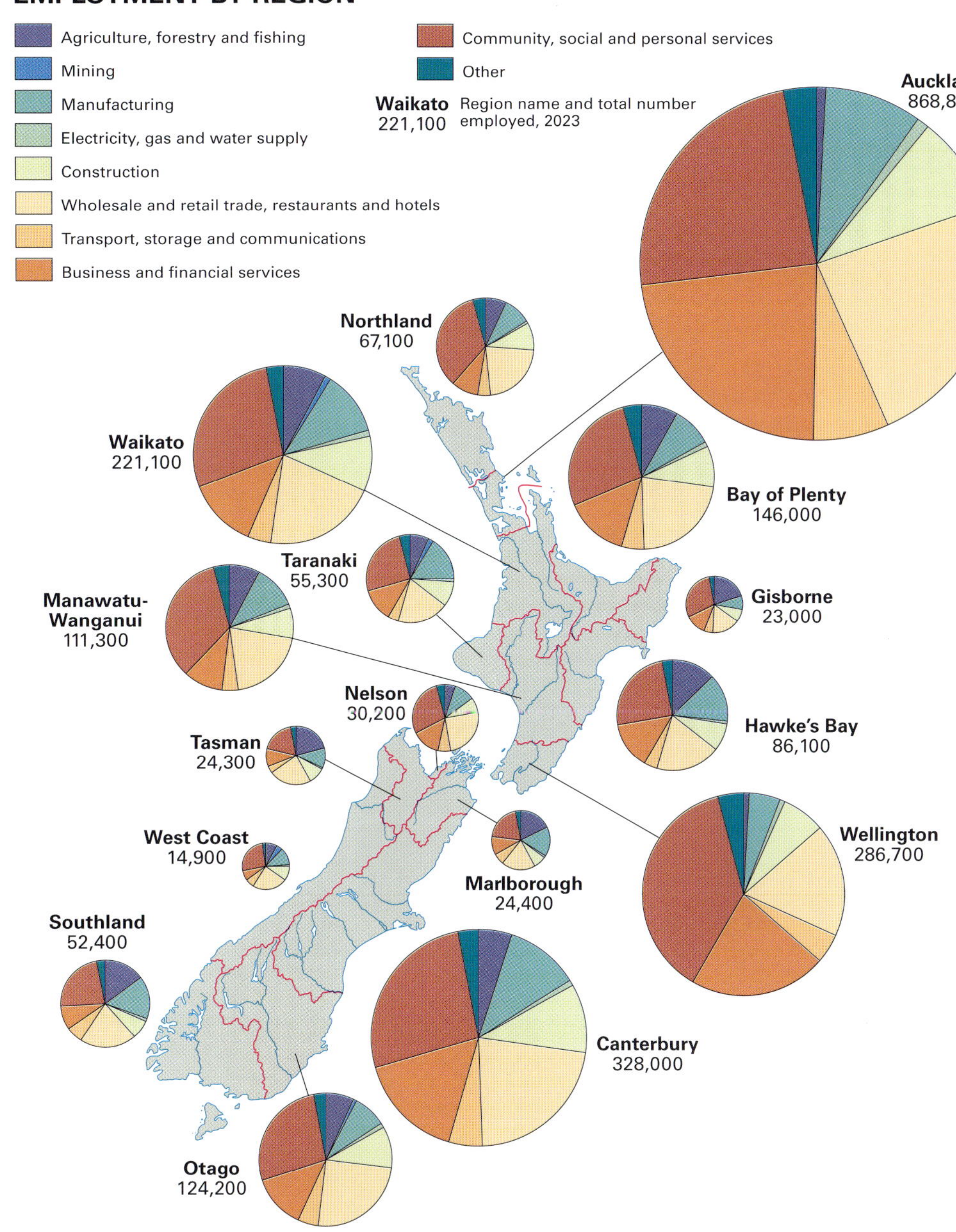

INTERNATIONAL TRADE

EXPORTS

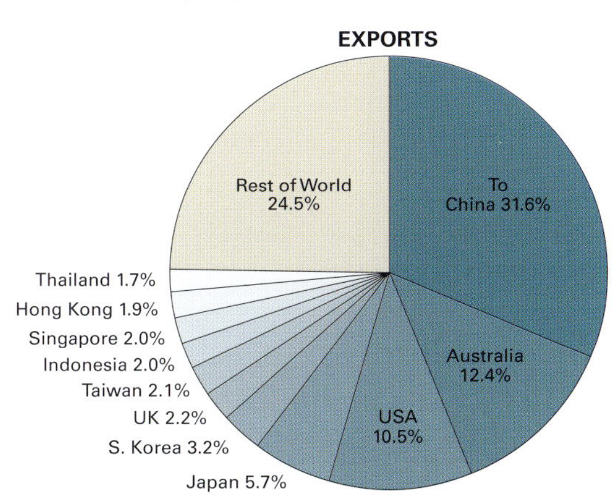

Value of total exports, 2021 : NZ$ 63,284 million
(of which dairy, eggs and honey products 27.6%, meat products 13.8% and wood products 8.7%)

IMPORTS

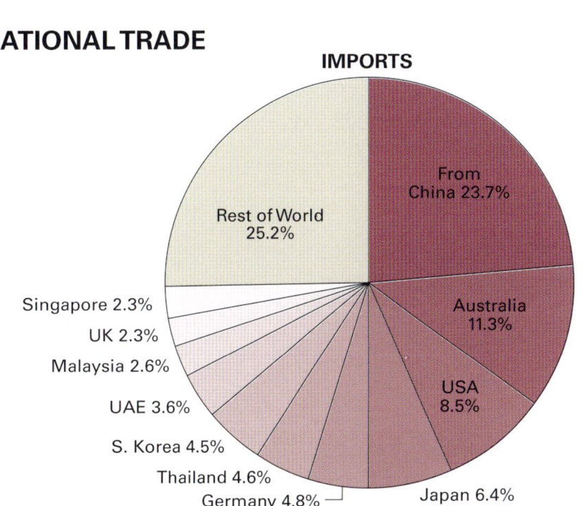

Value of total imports, 2021 : NZ$ 70,068 million
(of which vehicles 14.5%, machinery 8.8% and oil 7.9%)

NEW ZEALAND - NORTH ISLAND

1:3 500 000

1:3 500 000

National Parks

ISLANDS OF THE SOUTH-WEST PACIFIC

1:5 000 000

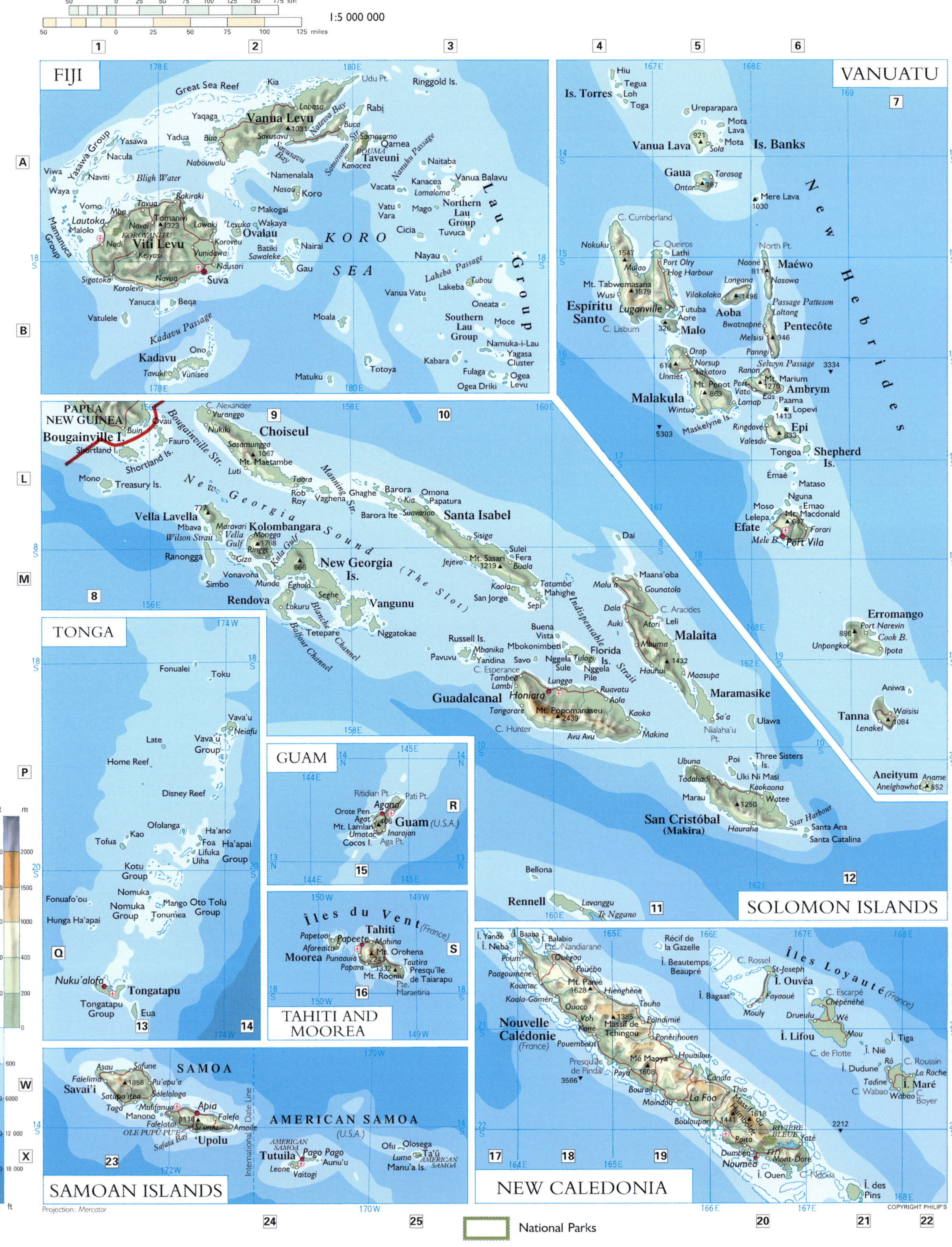

NEW ZEALAND INDEX

his index lists all the placenames which appear on the arge scale maps of New Zealand and the Southwest acific (pages which precede this index). Placenames for he rest of the world can be found in the index at the nd of the atlas.

he number in dark italics which follows each name in he index refers to the page number on which the place r feature is located. The letter and number which follow this indicate the section of the page where that place or feature can be found. Rivers are indexed to their mouths or confluences.

A solid square ■ follows the name of a country, while an open square □ shows that the name refers to a first order administrative district. An arrow → follows the name of a river. A triangle △ follows the name of a national park.

The alphabetic order of names composed of two or more words is governed by the first word and then by the second. Names composed of a proper name (Plenty) and a description (Bay of) are positioned alphabetically by the proper name. All names beginning St. are alphabetized under Saint and those beginning Mc under Mac.

bel Tasman △ 13 A8
but Hd. 13 D5
cheron → 13 C8
fareaitu 14 S16
ga Pt. 14 R15
gana 14 R15
gat 14 R15
haura → 13 C6
himanawa Ra. 12 F5
hipara B. 12 B2
huriri → 13 E5
jax, Mt. 13 C7
karoa 13 D7
karoa Harbour 13 D7
lbatross Pt. 12 E3
lexander, C. 14 L9
lexandra 13 F4
lfredton 12 G4
llanton 13 F5
maile 14 W24
mberley 13 D7
mbrym 14 F6
merican Samoa △ 14 X24
merican Samoa ■ 14 X24
name 14 K7
neityum 14 K7
nelghowhat 14 K7
nglem, Mt. 13 G2
niwa 14 J7
oba 14 E5
ola 14 M11
oraki/Mount Cook 13 D5
orangi Mts. 12 H4
ore 14 E5
otea Harbour 12 D3
otearoa = New Zealand ■ 12 G5
pia 14 W24
piti 12 F4
racides, C. 14 M11
ranga 12 B2
rapawa I. 13 B9
rapuni 12 E4
rawata → 13 F3
ria 12 E4
rrowsmith, Mt. 13 D5
rrowtown 13 E3
rthur's Pass 13 C6
rthur's Pass △ 13 C6
sau 14 W23
shburton 13 D6
shburton, North Branch → 13 D6
shburton, South Branch → 13 D6
shley → 13 D7
shurst 12 G4
spiring, Mt. 13 E3
thol 13 F3
tiamuri 12 E5
tori 14 M11
uckland 12 C3
uckland □ 12 C3
uki 14 M11
unu'u 14 X24
urora = Maéwo 14 E6
viemore, L. 13 E5
vu Avu 14 M11
wanui 12 B2
warua B. 13 E3
warua Pt. 13 E3
watere → 13 B9
aaba, Î. 14 T18
agaat, Î. 14 K4
alabio, Î. 14 T18
alclutha 13 G4
alfour Channel 14 M9
anks Is. 14 C5
anks Pen. 13 D8
arora 14 L10
arora Ite 14 L10
arrier, C. 12 C4
arrier Ra., *Otago, N.Z.* 13 E4
arrier Ra., *W. Coast, N.Z.* 13 E3
atiki 14 A2
ay of Plenty □ 12 D5
ay View 12 F5
eaumont 13 F4
eautemps-Beaupré, Î. 14 K4
elfast 13 D7
elgrove 13 B7
ellona 14 N10
en Ohau Ra. 13 E5
enmore Pk. 13 E5
eqa 14 B2
irchwood 13 F2
lackball 13 C6
lanche Channel 14 M9
lenheim 13 B8
ligh Sound 13 E2
ligh Water 14 A2
luff 13 G3
luff Harbour 13 G3
ougainville I. 14 L8
ougainville Str. 14 L9
ouloupari 14 U20
ouma △ 14 A2
ourail 14 U19
oyer, C. 14 U22
reaksea Sd. 13 F1
ream B. 12 B3
ream Hd. 12 B3
Bream Tail 12 C3
Brett, C. 12 B3
Brightwater 13 B8
Bruce B. 13 D4
Brunner, L. 13 C6
Bua 14 A2
Buala 14 M10
Buca 14 A2
Buena Vista 14 M11
Buin 14 L8
Buller → 13 B6
Buller Gorge 13 B7
Bulls 12 G4
Bunnythorpe 12 G4
Bwatnapné 14 E6
Cambridge 12 D4
Cameron Mts. 13 G1
Campbell, C. 13 B9
Campbelltown = Bluff 13 G3
Canala 14 U19
Canterbury □ 13 D6
Canterbury Bight 13 E6
Canterbury Plains 13 D6
Caroline Pk. 13 F2
Carterton 12 H4
Cascade Pt. 13 E3
Castlecliff 12 F4
Castlepoint 12 G5
Caswell Sound 13 E2
Cavalli Is. 12 B2
Chalky Inlet 13 G1
Charles Sound 13 F2
Chaslands Mistake 13 G4
Chatham I. 13 a
Chatham Is. 13 a
Chépénéhé 14 K5
Choiseul 14 L9
Christchurch 13 D7
Cicia 14 A3
Clarence → 13 C8
Clifden 13 G2
Clinton 13 G4
Clive 12 F5
Cloudy B. 13 B9
Clutha → 13 G4
Clyde 13 F4
Coal I. 13 G1
Cocos I. 14 R15
Codfish I. 13 G2
Coleridge, L. 13 D6
Collingwood 13 A7
Colville, C. 12 C4
Cook, Mt. = Aoraki/Mount Cook 13 D5
Cook B. 14 H7
Cook Strait 12 H3
Coromandel 12 C4
Coromandel Pen. 12 C4
Coromandel Ra. 12 C4
Cromwell 13 F4
Crossley, Mt. 13 C7
Culverden 13 C7
Cumberland, C. 14 D4
Cuvier I. 12 C4
Dagg Sd. 13 F1
Dai 14 L11
Dala 14 M11
Dannevirke 12 G5
Darfield 13 D7
Dargaville 12 B2
Darran Mts. 13 E2
Devil River Pk. 13 A7
Dipton 13 F3
Disney Reef 14 P13
Dometti 13 C8
Donnelly's Crossing 12 B2
Double Cone 13 F3
Doubtful Sd. 13 F1
Doubtless B. 12 A2
Doughboy B. 13 H2
Drueulu 14 K5
Dudune, Î. 14 U21
Dumbéa 14 V20
Dunback 13 F5
Dunedin 13 F5
Dunstan Mts. 13 E4
Duntroon 13 E5
D'Urville I. 13 A8
Dusky Sd. 13 F1
Earnslaw, Mt. 13 E3
Eas 14 F6
East C. 12 D7
Eastbourne 12 H3
Eastern Group = Lau Group 14 A3
Edendale 13 G3
Edgecumbe 12 D5
Edievale 13 F4
Efate 14 G6
Efate, I. 14 G6
Egholo 14 M9
Egmont △ 12 F3
Egmont, C. 12 F2
Egmont, Mt. = Taranaki, Mt. 12 F3
Eketahuna 12 G4
Ellesmere, L. 13 H7
Eltham 12 F3
Émaé 14 G6
Emao 14 G6
Epi 14 F6
Erromango 14 H7
Escarpé, C. 14 K5
Esperance, C. 14 M10
Espiritu Santo 14 E4
Eua 14 Q13
Eyre Mts. 13 F3
Fairlie 13 E5
Falefa 14 W24
Falelatai 14 W24
Falelima 14 W23
Farewell, C. 13 A7
Farewell Spit 13 A8
Fauro 14 L9
Fayaoué 14 K4
Featherston 12 H4
Feilding 12 G4
Fera 14 M10
Fiji ■ 14 A2
Fiordland △ 13 F2
Flat Pt. 12 H4
Florida Is. 14 M11
Flotte, C. de 14 U21
Foa 14 P13
Fonuafo'ou 14 Q13
Fonualei 14 P13
Forari 14 G6
Forsyth I. 13 A9
Fortrose 13 G3
Foulwind, C. 13 B6
Foveaux Str. 13 G3
Foxton 12 G4
Franklin Mts. 13 E2
Franklyn Mt. 13 C7
Frasertown 12 E6
French Pass 13 A8
Friendly Is. = Tonga ■ 14 P13
Fulaga 14 B3
Galatea 12 E5
Garvie Mts. 13 F3
Gau 14 B2
Gaua 14 D5
Gazelle, Récif de la 14 T19
George Sound 13 E2
Geraldine 13 E6
Ghaghe 14 L10
Gillespies Pt. 13 D4
Gisborne 12 E7
Gisborne □ 12 E6
Gizo 14 M9
Glen Afton 12 D4
Glen Massey 12 D4
Glenavy 13 E6
Glenham 13 G3
Glenhope 13 B7
Glenmary, Mt. 13 D4
Glenorchy 13 E3
Golden B. 13 A7
Gore 13 G3
Gounatolo 14 M11
Granity 13 B6
Great Barrier I. 12 C4
Great Sea Reef 14 A2
Grey → 13 C6
Greymouth 13 C6
Greytown 12 H4
Guadalcanal 14 M11
Guam ■ 14 R15
Ha'ano 14 P13
Ha'apai Group 14 P13
Haast 13 D4
Haast → 13 D4
Haast Pass 13 D4
Hakataramea 13 E5
Halcombe 12 G4
Halfmoon Bay 13 G3
Hamilton 12 D4
Hampden 13 F5
Hanmer Springs 13 C7
Harihari 13 D5
Harris Mts. 13 E3
Hastings 12 F5
Hauhui 14 M11
Hauhungaroa Ra. 12 E4
Hauraha 14 N11
Hauraki G. 12 C4
Hauroko L. 13 F2
Havelock 13 B8
Havelock North 12 F5
Hawea, L. 13 E4
Hawea Flat 13 E4
Hawera 12 F3
Hawkdun Ra. 13 E5
Hawke B. 12 F6
Hawke's Bay □ 12 F5
Heath Mts. 13 F2
Hedgehope 13 G3
Helensville 12 C3
Hen and Chickens Is. 12 B3
Herbertville 12 G5
Herekino 12 B2
Hicks Bay 12 D7
Hienghène 14 T18
Highbank 13 D6
Hikurangi, *Gisborne, N.Z.* 12 E5
Hikurangi, *Northland, N.Z.* 12 B3
Hinds 13 D6
Hiu 14 C4
Hog Harbour 14 E5
Hokianga Harbour 12 B2
Hokitika 13 C5
Home Reef 14 P13
Honiara 14 M10
Hornby 13 D7
Houailou 14 U19
Houhora Heads 12 A2
Howick 12 C3
Huiarau Ra. 12 E5
Huiroa 12 F3
Humboldt, Massif du 14 U20
Humboldt Mts. 13 E3
Hunga Ha'apai 14 Q13
Hunter 13 E6
Hunter → 13 E4
Hunter, C. 14 M10
Hunter Hills, The 13 E5
Hunter Mts. 13 F2
Hunterville 12 F4
Huntly 12 D4
Hurunui → 13 C8
Hyde 13 F5
Ikamatua 13 C6
Inangahua 13 B6
Inarajan 14 R15
Indispensable Strait 14 M11
Inglewood 12 F3
Inland Kaikoura Ra. 13 B8
Invercargill 13 G3
Ipota 14 H7
Islands, B. of 12 B3
Jackson, C. 13 A9
Jackson B. 13 D3
Jackson Hd. 13 D3
Jacksons 13 C6
Jane Pk. 13 F3
Jejevo 14 M10
Johnsonville 12 H3
Kaala-Gomén 14 T18
Kabara 14 B3
Kadavu 14 B2
Kadavu Passage 14 B2
Kaeo 12 B2
Kaherekoau Mts. 13 F2
Kahurangi △ 13 B7
Kahurangi Pt. 13 A7
Kaiapoi 13 D7
Kaikohe 12 B2
Kaikoura 13 C8
Kaikoura Pen. 13 C8
Kaimanawa Mts. 12 F4
Kaimata 13 C6
Kaipara Harbour 12 C3
Kaitaia 12 B2
Kaitangata 13 G4
Kakanui Mts. 13 F5
Kamo 12 B3
Kanacea, *Lau Group, Fiji* 14 A3
Kanacea, *Taveuni, Fiji* 14 A2
Kandavu = Kadavu 14 B2
Kandavu Passage = Kadavu Passage 14 B2
Kaniere, L. 13 C6
Kao 14 P13
Kaoka 14 M11
Kaokaona 14 N11
Kaolo 14 M10
Kapiti I. 12 G3
Kaponga 12 F3
Kapuni 12 F3
Karamea 13 B7
Karamea → 13 B7
Karamea Bight 13 B6
Karapiro 12 D4
Karikari, C. 12 A2
Katikati 12 D4
Kawakawa 12 B3
Kawau I. 12 C3
Kaweka Ra. 12 F5
Kawerau 12 E5
Kawhia 12 E3
Kawhia Harbour 12 E3
Keiyasi 14 A1
Kelso 13 F4
Kepler Mts. 13 F2
Kerikeri 12 B2
Kia, *Fiji* 14 A2
Kia, *Solomon Is.* 14 L10
Kidnappers, C. 12 F6
Kihikihi 12 E4
Kingston 13 F3
Kinleith 12 E4
Kirikopuni 12 B3
Kirkliston Ra. 13 E5
Kohukohu 12 B2
Kolombangara 14 M9
Koné 14 U18
Koro 14 A2
Koro Sea 14 A3
Korolevu 14 B1
Korovou 14 A2
Koroyanitu △ 14 A1
Kotu Group 14 Q14
Koumac 14 T18
Kula Gulf 14 M9
Kumara 13 C6
Kurow 13 E5
La Foa 14 U19
La Roche 14 U22
Labasa 14 A2
Lakatoro 14 F5
Lake Coleridge 13 D6
Lake Pukaki 13 E5
Lake Tekapo 13 D5
Lakeba 14 B3
Lakeba Passage 14 B3
Lakemba = Lakeba 14 B3
Lamap 14 F5
Lambasa = Labasa 14 A2
Lambi 14 M10
Lamlan, Mt. 14 R15
Late 14 P13
Lathi 14 D5
Lau Group 14 A3
Lautoka 14 A1
Lavanggu 14 N11
Lawaki 14 A2
Lawrence 13 F4
Leamington 12 D4
Leeston 13 D7
Lelepa 14 G6
Leli 14 M11
Lenakel 14 J7
Leone 14 X24
Levin 12 G4
Levuka 14 A2
Lewis Pass 13 C7
Lifou, I. 14 K5
Lifuka 14 P13
Lincoln 13 D7
Lisburn, C. 14 E4
Little Barrier I. 12 C4
Little River 13 D7
Livingstone Mts. 13 F3
Loh 14 C4
Lokuru 14 M9
Loltong 14 E6
Lomaloma 14 A3
Long Pt. 13 G4
Longana 14 E5
Longburn 12 G4
Lopevi 14 F6
Lower Hutt 12 H3
Loyalty Is. = Loyauté, Îs. 14 K4
Loyauté, Îs. 14 K4
Luganville 14 E5
Luma 14 X25
Lumsden 13 F3
Lungga 14 M11
Luti 14 L9
Lyall Mt. 13 F2
Lyell 13 B7
Lyttelton 13 D7
Maana'oba 14 M11
Maasupa 14 M11
Macdonald, Mt. 14 G6
Mackenzie Plains 13 E5
McKerrow, L. 13 E3
Maetambe, Mt. 14 L9
Maéwo 14 E6
Mago 14 A3
Maheno 13 F5
Mahia Pen. 12 F6
Mahighe 14 M10
Mahina 14 S16
Makarewa 13 G3
Makina 14 M11
Makogai 14 A2
Malaita 14 M11
Malakula 14 F5
Mallicolo = Malakula 14 F5
Malo 14 E5
Malolo 14 A1
Malu'a 14 M11
Mamaku 12 E5
Mamanuca Group 14 A1
Manaia 12 F3
Manakau 13 C8
Manapouri 13 F2
Manapouri, L. 13 F2
Manawatu → 12 G4
Manawatu-Wanganui □ 12 F4
Mangakino 12 E4
Mangaweka 12 F4
Mangaweka, Mt. 12 F5
Mango 14 Q14
Mangonui 12 B2
Manning Str. 14 L10
Manono 14 W23
Manu'a Is. 14 X25
Manukau 12 D3
Manukau Harbour 12 D3
Manunui 12 E4
Manuoha 12 E6
Mapourika, L. 13 D5
Maraetiria, Pte. 14 S16
Maramasike 14 M11
Marau 14 N11
Maravari 14 L9
Maré, Î. 14 U22
Maria van Diemen, C. 12 A1
Marium, Mt. 14 F6
Marlborough □ 13 B8
Martinborough 12 H4
Marton 12 G4
Maruia → 13 B7
Maskelyne Is. 14 F5
Mason B. 13 G2
Masterton 12 G4
Matakana 12 C3
Matamata 12 D4
Mataso 14 G6
Matata 12 D5
Mataura 13 G3
Mataura → 13 G3
Matiri Ra. 13 B7
Matuku 14 B2
Maungaturoto 12 C3
Mauriceville 12 G4
Maxwell 12 F3
Mayor I. 12 D5
Mba 14 A1
Mbanika 14 M10
Mbava 14 L9
Mbengga = Beqa 14 B2
Mbokonimbeti 14 M11
Mbuma 14 M11
Mé Maoya 14 U19
Mele B. 14 G6
Melsisi 14 E6
Mercer 12 D4
Mercury B. 12 C4
Mercury Is. 12 C4
Mere Lava 14 D6
Methven 13 D6
Middlemarch 13 F5
Midhirst 12 F3
Milford Sd. 13 E2
Miller's Flat 13 F4
Millerton 13 B6
Milton 13 G4
Mitre, Mt. 12 G4
Moala 14 B2
Moce 14 B3
Moerewa 12 B3
Mohaka → 12 F6
Moindou 14 U19
Mokai 12 E4
Mokau 12 E3
Mokau → 12 E3
Mokihinui → 13 B6
Molesworth 13 C8
Mongga 14 L9
Mono 14 L8
Monowai 13 F2
Monowai, L. 13 F2
Mont-Dore 14 V20
Montohora 12 E6
Mooréa 14 S16
Morrinsville 12 D4
Morven 13 E6
Mosgiel 13 F5
Moso 14 G6
Mossburn 13 F3
Mota 14 C5
Mota Lava 14 C5
Motiti I. 12 D5
Motu → 12 D6
Motueka 13 B8
Motueka → 13 B8
Mou 14 U19
Mouly 14 K4
Mount Aspiring △ 13 E3
Mount Cook 13 D5
Mount Cook △ 13 D5
Mount Maunganui 12 D5
Mount Somers 13 D6
Mount Wellington 12 C3
Moutohara 12 E6
Mulifanua 14 W24
Munda 14 M9
Murchison 13 B7
Murchison, Mt. 13 D6
Murchison Mts. 13 F2
Muriwai Beach 12 C3
Murupara 12 E5
Nabouwalu 14 A2
Nacula 14 A1
Nadi 14 A1
Nairai 14 A2
Naitaba 14 A3
Nambouwalu = Nabouwalu 14 A2
Namenalala 14 A2
Namuka-i-Lau 14 B3
Nandi = Nadi 14 A1
Nandiarane, Pte. 14 T18
Nanuku Passage 14 A3
Naoné 14 E6
Napier 12 F5
Nasau 14 A2
Nasawa 14 E6
Naseby 13 F5
Natewa B. 14 A2
Nausori 14 B2
Navai 14 A1
Naviti 14 A1
Navua 14 B2
Nayau 14 B2
Ndoua, C. 14 V20
Neba, Î. 14 T17
Needles Pt. 12 C4
Neiafu 14 P14
Nelson 13 B8
Nelson □ 13 B8
Nelson Lakes △ 13 B7
New Brighton 13 D7
New Caledonia ■ 14 U19
New Georgia Is. 14 M9
New Georgia Sound 14 L9
New Hebrides = Vanuatu ■ 14 E6
New Plymouth 12 F3
New Zealand ■ 12 G5
Ngapara 13 E5
Ngaruawahia 12 D4
Ngaruroro → 12 F5
Ngatapa 12 E6
Ngauruhoe, Mt. 12 F4
Nggatokae 14 M10
Nggela 14 M11
Nggela Pile 14 M11
Nggela Sule 14 M11
Ngongotaha 12 E5
Nguna 14 G6
Nialaha'u Pt. 14 M11
Niē, Î. 14 U21
Nightcaps 13 F3
Ninety Mile Beach 12 A1
Nokuku 14 D4
Nomuka 14 Q13
Nomuka Group 14 Q13
Normanby 12 F3
Norsewood 12 G5
Norsup 14 F5
North C. 12 A2
North I. 12 E4
North Pt. 14 D6
North Taranaki Bight 12 E3
Northern Lau Group 14 A3
Northland □ 12 B2
Nouméa 14 V20
Nouvelle-Calédonie = New Caledonia ■ 14 U19
Nugget Pt. 13 G4
Nuhaka 12 F6
Nukiki 14 L9
Nuku'alofa 14 Q14
O Le Pupū Pu'e △ 14 W24
Oamaru 13 F5
Ofolanga 14 P14
Ofu 14 X25
Ogea Driki 14 B3
Ogea Levu 14 B3
Ohai 13 F3
Ohakune 12 F4
Ohau, L. 13 E4
Ohaupo 12 D4
Ohiwa Harbour 12 D6
Ohura 12 E3
Okahukura 12 E4
Okaihau 12 B2
Okarito 13 D5
Okato 12 F2
Okuru 13 D3
Olivine Ra. 13 E3
Olosega 14 X25
Omapere 12 B2
Omona 14 L10
Oneata 14 B3
Onehunga 12 C3
Onerahi 12 B3
Ongarue 12 E4
Ongea Levu = Ogea Levu 14 B3
Ono 14 B2
Onoke, L. 12 H4
Ontar 14 D5
Opapa 12 F5
Opotiki 12 E6
Opua 12 B3
Opunake 12 F2
Orap 14 E5
Orawia 13 G2
Orepuki 13 G2
Oreti → 13 G3
Ormond 12 E6
Ormondville 12 G5
Orohena, Mt. 14 S16
Orote Pen. 14 R15
Ostend 12 C4
Otago □ 13 E4
Otago Harbour 13 F5
Otago Pen. 13 F5
Otahuhu 12 C3
Otaki 12 G4
Otane 12 F5
Ōtautahi = Christchurch 13 D7
Otautau 13 G3
Ōtepoti = Dunedin 13 F5
Otira 13 C6
Otira Gorge 13 C6
Oto Tolu Group 14 Q13
Otorohanga 12 E4
Ouaco 14 T18
Ouégoa 14 T18
Ouen, Î. 14 V20
Ouvéa, Î. 14 K4
Ovalau 14 A2
Ovau 14 L9
Owaka 13 G4
Owen, Mt. 13 B7
Owhango 12 F4
Oxford 13 D7
Paagoumène 14 T18
Paama 14 F6
Paekakariki 12 G3
Paengaroa 12 D5
Paeroa 12 D4
Pago Pago 14 X24
Pahia Pt. 13 G2
Pahiatua 12 G4
Paihia 12 B3
Paīta 14 V20
Palliser, C. 12 H4
Palliser B. 12 H4
Palmerston 13 F5
Palmerston North 12 G4
Panié, Mt. 14 T18
Panngi 14 E6
Papakura 12 D3
Papara 14 S16
Paparoa 12 C3
Paparoa △ 13 C6
Paparoa Ra. 13 C6
Papatoetoe 12 C3
Papatura 14 L10
Papeete 14 S16
Papetoai 14 S16
Paraparaumu 12 G4
Parengarenga Harbour 12 A1
Parnassus 13 C8
Patea 12 F3
Paterson Inlet 13 G3
Pati Pt. 14 R15
Patteson, Passage 14 E6
Pauanui 12 D4
Pavuvu 14 M10
Pegasus Bay 13 D8
Pelorus → 13 B8
Pelorus Sd. 13 A8
Penot, Mt. 14 F5
Pentecost = Pentecôte 14 E6
Pentecôte 14 E6
Petone 12 H3
Piako → 12 D4
Picton 13 B9
Piha 12 C3
Pindaï, Presqu'île de 14 U18
Pins, Î. des 14 V21
Pipiriki 12 F4
Pisa Ra. 13 E4
Pitt I. 13 a
Pleasant Point 13 E6
Plenty, B. of 12 D6
Poi 14 N11
Poindimié 14 T19
Ponérihouen 14 U19
Poor Knights Is. 12 B3
Popomanaseu, Mt. 14 M11
Porangahau 12 G5
Port Chalmers 13 F5
Port Charles 12 C4
Port Fitzroy 12 C4
Port Narevin 14 H7
Port Nicholson 12 H3
Port Olry 14 E5
Port Pegasus 13 H2
Port Vato 14 F6
Port Vila 14 G6
Portland I. 12 F6
Poteriteri, L. 13 G2
Pouébo 14 T18
Pouembout 14 U18
Poum 14 T18
Poverty B. 12 E7
Poya 14 U19
Preservation Inlet 13 G1
Providence, C. 13 F1
Pu'apu'a 14 W23
Puha 12 E6
Pukaki, L. 13 E5
Pukearuhe 12 E3
Pukekohe 12 D3
Puketeraki Ra. 13 C7
Puketoi Ra. 12 G5
Pukeuri 13 F6
Punaauia 14 S16
Putaruru 12 E4
Putorino 12 F5
Pututahi 12 E6
Puysegur Pt. 13 G1
Qamea 14 A3
Queen Charlotte Sd. 13 B9
Queenstown 13 F3
Queiros, C. 14 D5
Rabi 14 A3
Raetihi 12 F4
Raglan 12 D3
Raglan Harbour 12 D3
Rahotu 12 F2
Rakaia 13 D7
Rakaia → 13 D7
Rakiraki 14 A2
Rambi = Rabi 14 A3
Ranfurly 13 F5
Rangataua 12 F4
Rangaunu B. 12 A2
Rangiora 13 D7
Rangitaiki 12 E5
Rangitaiki → 12 D5
Rangitata → 13 D6
Rangitikei → 12 G4
Rangitoto ke te tonga = D'Urville I. 13 A8
Rangitoto Ra. 12 E4
Ranon 14 F6
Ranongga 14 M9
Raukumara Ra. 12 E6
Rawene 12 B2
Reefton 13 C6
Reinga, C. 12 A1
Rekohua = Chatham I. 13 a
Remarkables, The 13 F3
Rendova 14 M9
Rennell 14 N11
Renwick 13 B8
Resolution I. 13 F1
Riccarton 13 D7
Richardson Mts. 13 E3
Richmond 13 B8
Richmond, Mt. 13 B8
Richmond Ra. 13 B8
Ringdove 14 F6
Ringgi 14 M9
Ringgold Is. 14 A3
Ritidian Pt. 14 R15
Riversdale 13 F3
Riverton 13 G2
Rivière Bleue △ 14 V20
Riwaka 13 B7
Rô 14 U21
Rob Roy 14 L9
Rodney, C. 12 C3
Rolleston 13 D7
Rongotea 12 G4
Rooniu, Mt. 14 S16
Ross 13 C5
Rossel, C. 14 K4
Rotoaira, L. 12 F4
Rotoehu, L. 12 E5
Rotoiti, L., *Bay of Plenty, N.Z.* 12 E5
Rotoiti, L., *W. Coast, N.Z.* 13 B7
Rotoma, L. 12 E5
Rotoroa, L. 13 B7
Rotorua 12 E5
Rotorua, L. 12 E5
Rough Ridge 13 F4
Roussin, C. 14 U21
Roxburgh 13 F4
Ruahine Ra. 12 F5
Ruamahanga → 12 H4
Ruapehu 12 F4
Ruapuke I. 13 G3
Ruatoria 12 D7
Ruavatu 14 M11
Ruawai 12 C2
Runanga 13 C6
Runaway, C. 12 D6
Russell 12 B3
Russell Is. 14 M10
Sa'a 14 M11
Safata B. 14 X24
Safune 14 W23
St. Andrews 13 E6
St. Arnaud Ra. 13 C7
St. Bathans 13 E4
St. Bathan's, Mt. 13 E4
St-Joseph 14 K4
St. Kilda 13 F5
Salelologa 14 W23
Samoa ■ 14 X24
Samoan Is. 14 X24
San Cristóbal 14 N11
San Jorge 14 M10
Santa Ana 14 N12
Santa Catalina 14 N12
Santa Isabel 14 M10
Sasamungga 14 L9
Sasari, Mt. 14 M10
Satupa'itea 14 W23
Saunders, C. 13 F5
Savai'i 14 W23
Savo 14 M10
Savusavu 14 A2
Savusavu B. 14 A2
Sawaleke 14 A2
Scargill 13 C7
Seaward Kaikoura Ra. 13 C8
Secretary I. 13 F1
Seddon 13 B9
Seddonville 13 B7
Sefton 13 D7
Seghe 14 M9
Selwyn Passage 14 F6
Separation Pt. 13 A7
Sepi 14 M10
Shag Pt. 13 F5
Shannon 12 G4
Sheffield 13 D7
Shepherd Is. 14 F6
Shortland I. 14 L8
Shortland Is. 14 L8
Shotover → 13 E3
Sigatoka 14 B1
Simbo 14 M9
Singatoka = Sigatoka 14 B1
Sisiga 14 L10
Si'umu 14 X24
Slot, The = New Georgia Sound 14 L9
Snells Beach 12 C3
Sola 14 C5
Solander I. 13 G1
Solomon Is. ■ 14 L8
Somosomo 14 A3
Somosomo Str. 14 A3
South I. 13 E5
South Invercargill 13 G3
South Taranaki Bight 12 F3
South West C. 13 H2
Southbridge 13 D7
Southern Alps 13 D5
Southern Lau Group 14 B3
Southland □ 13 F3
Spenser Mts. 13 C7
Springfield 13 D6
Star Harbour 14 N12
Stephens, C. 13 A8
Stephens I. 13 A9
Stewart I. 13 G2
Stirling 13 G4
Stoke 13 B8
Stratford 12 F3
Stuart Mts. 13 F2
Studholme 13 E6
Suavanao 14 L10
Sulei 14 M10
Sumner 13 D7
Sumner, L. 13 C7

Sutherland Falls 13 E2
Sutton 13 F5
Suva 14 B2
Table C. 12 F7
Tabwemasana, Mt. 14 E4
Tadahadi 14 N11
Tadine 14 U21
Tadmor 13 B7
Taga 14 W23
Tahakopa 13 G4
Tahiti 14 S16
Tahora 12 F3
Taiarapu, Presq. de 14 S16
Taieri → 13 G5
Taihape 12 F4
Tairua 12 D4
Takaka 13 A7
Takapau 12 G5
Takapuna 12 C3
Tāmaki-makau-rau = Auckland 12 C3
Tambea 14 M10
Taneatua 12 E6
Tangarare 14 M10
Tangariro, Mt. 12 F4
Tanna 14 J7
Taora 14 L9
Tapanui 13 F4
Tapuae-o-Uenuku 13 B8
Taradale 12 F5
Taramakau → 13 C6
Taranaki □ 12 F3
Taranaki, Mt. 12 F3
Tararua Ra. 12 G4
Tarasag 14 D5
Tarawera 12 F5
Tarawera, L. 12 E5
Tarawera, Mt. 12 E5
Tasman □ 13 B7
Tasman → 13 D5
Tasman, Mt. 13 D5
Tasman B. 13 A8
Tasman Mts. 13 B7
Tatamba 14 M10
Ta'ū 14 X25
Taumarunui 12 E4
Taupo 12 E5
Taupo, L. 12 E4
Tauranga 12 D5
Tauranga Harb. 12 D5
Tauroa Pt. 12 B2
Tautira 14 S16
Taveuni 14 A3
Tavua 14 A1
Tavuki 14 B2
Taylor, Mt. 13 D6
Tchingou, Massif de 14 T19
Te Anau 13 F2
Te Anau, L. 13 F2
Te Araroa 12 D7
Te Aroha 12 D4
Te Awamutu 12 E4
Te Ika a Maui = North I. 12 E4
Te Kaha 12 D6
Te Karaka 12 E6
Te Kauwhata 12 D4
Te Kopuru 12 C2
Te Kuiti 12 E4
Te Puke 12 D5
Te Teko 12 E5
Te Waewae B. 13 G2
Te Wai Pounamu = South I. 13 E5
Te Whanganui-a-Tara = Wellington 12 H3
Tegua 14 C4
Tekapo → 13 E5
Tekapo, L. 13 D5
Temuka 13 E6
Terawhiti, C. 12 H3
Tetepare 14 M9
Thames 12 D4
Thames, Firth of 12 D4
Thio 14 U20
Thithia = Cicia 14 A3
Thompson Sd. 13 F1
Thornbury 13 G3
Three Sisters Is. 14 N11
Thy △ 14 V20
Tiga, Î. 14 U21
Timaru 13 E6
Tinui 12 G5
Tinwald 13 D6
Tirau 12 D4
Tiritiri o te Moana = Southern Alps 13 D5
Tirua Pt. 12 E3
Tititira Hd. 13 D4
Toetoes B. 13 G3
Tofua 14 P13
Toga 14 C4
Tokaanu 12 E4
Tokanui 13 G3
Tokarahi 13 E5
Tokomaru Bay 12 E7
Tokoroa 12 E4
Toku 14 P13
Tolaga Bay 12 E7
Tomanlivi 14 A2
Tonga ■ 14 P13
Tongariro △ 12 F4
Tongatapu 14 Q14
Tongatapu Group 14 Q13
Tongoa 14 F6
Tonumea 14 Q13
Torres, Is. 14 C4
Totoya, I. 14 B3
Touho 14 T19
Travers, Mt. 13 C7
Treasury Is. 14 L8
Tryphena 12 C4
Tuaheni Pt. 12 E7
Tuai 12 E6
Tuakau 12 D3
Tuamarina 13 B8
Tuatapere 13 G2
Tubou 14 B3
Tukituki → 12 F5
Tulagi 14 M11
Turakina 12 G4
Turakina → 12 G4
Turakirae Hd. 12 H3
Turangi 12 E4
Turnagain, C. 12 G5
Turua 12 D4
Tutuba 14 E5
Tutuila 14 X24
Tutuko, Mt. 13 E3
Tuvuca 14 A3
Two Thumb Ra. 13 D5
Ubuna 14 N11
Udu Pt. 14 A3
Uiha 14 P13
Uki Ni Masi 14 N11
Ulawa 14 M11
Umatac 14 R15
Umbrella Mts. 13 F4
Unmet 14 F5
Unpongkor 14 H6
'Upolu 14 W24
Upper Hutt 12 H4
Ureparapara 14 C5
Urewera △ 12 E6
Vacata 14 A3
Vaghena 14 L9
Vaitogi 14 X24
Valesdir 14 F6
Vangunu 14 M10
Vanua Balavu 14 A3
Vanua Lava 14 C5
Vanua Levu 14 A2
Vanua Vatu 14 B3
Vanuatu ■ 14 E6
Vaté = Efate, I. 14 G6
Vatu Vara 14 A3
Vatulele 14 B1
Vava'u 14 P14
Vava'u Group 14 P14
Vella G. 14 M9
Vella Lavella 14 L9
Vent, Îs. du 14 S16
Victoria, Mt. = Tomanlivi 14 A2
Victoria Ra. 13 C7
Vilakalaka 14 E5
Viti Levu 14 A1
Viwa 14 A1
Voh 14 T18
Vomo 14 A1
Vonavona 14 M9
Vunidawa 14 A2
Vunisea 14 B2
Vuranggo 14 L9
Wabao 14 U21
Wabao, C. 14 U21
Waharoa 12 D4
Waiapu → 12 D7
Waiau 13 C8
Waiau →, *Canterbury, N.Z.* 13 C8
Waiau →, *Southland, N.Z.* 13 G2
Waihao → 13 E6
Waihao Downs 13 E5
Waiheke I. 12 C4
Waihi 12 D4
Waihi Beach 12 D7
Waihola 13 G5
Waihola L. 13 F5
Waihou → 12 D4
Waikaia 13 F3
Waikaka 13 F4
Waikare, L. 12 D4
Waikareiti, L. 12 E6
Waikaremoana 12 E6
Waikaremoana, L. 12 E6
Waikari 13 C7
Waikato → 12 D3
Waikiekie 12 B3
Waikokopu 12 F6
Waikouaiti 13 F5
Waikouaiti Downs 13 F5
Waimakariri → 13 D7
Waimangaroa 13 B6
Waimarie 13 B6
Waimate 13 E6
Waimea Plain 13 F3
Wainuiomata 12 H3
Waiotapu 12 E5
Waiouru 12 F4
Waipa → 12 E4
Waipahi 13 G4
Waipapa Pt. 13 G3
Waipara 13 D7
Waipawa 12 F5
Waipiro 12 E7
Waipiro Bay 12 E7
Waipoua Forest 12 B2
Waipu 12 B3
Waipukurau 12 G5
Wairakei 12 E5
Wairarapa, L. 12 H4
Wairau → 13 B9
Wairio 13 F3
Wairoa 12 F6
Wairoa →, *Hawke's Bay, N.Z.* 12 F6
Wairoa →, *Northland, N.Z.* 12 C2
Waïsisi 14 J7
Waitaki → 13 E6
Waitaki Plains 13 E5
Waitangi 12 B3
Waitara 12 E3
Waitara → 12 E3
Waitoa 12 D4
Waitomo Caves 12 E4
Waitotara 12 F3
Waitotara → 12 F3
Waiuku 12 D3
Wakatipu, L. 13 F3
Wakaya 14 A2
Wakefield 13 B8
Wallacetown 13 G3
Wanaka 13 E4
Wanaka, L. 13 E4
Wanganui 12 F4
Wanganui →, *W. Coast, N.Z.* 13 D5
Wanganui →, *Wanganui-Manawatu, N.Z.* 12 F4
Wanstead 12 G5
Ward 13 B9
Warkworth 12 C3
Warrington 13 F5
Watee 14 N12
Waverley 12 F3
Waya 14 A1
Wé 14 K5
Weber 12 G5
Wellington 12 H3
Wellington □ 12 G4
Wellsford 12 C3
West Coast □ 13 D5
Western Samoa = Samoa ■ 14 X24
Westland △ 13 D5
Westland Bight 13 C5
Westport 13 B6
Whakaari = White I. 12 D6
Whakamaru 12 E4
Whakatane 12 D6
Whakatane → 12 D6
Whangaehu → 12 G4
Whangamata 12 D4
Whangamomona 12 F3
Whanganui △ 12 F3
Whangaparaoa Pen. 12 C4
Whangarei 12 B3
Whangarei Harb. 12 B3
Whangaroa Harb. 12 B2
Whangaruru Harb. 12 B3
Wharanui 13 B9
Wharekauri = Chatham Is. 13 a
Whataroa 13 D5
Whataroa → 13 D5
Whitcombe Pass 13 D5
White I. 12 D6
Whitecliffs 13 D6
Whitianga 12 C4
Wilson Str. 14 M9
Winchester 13 E6
Windsor 13 E5
Winton 13 G3
Wintua 14 F5
Woodville 12 G4
Wusi 14 E4
Wyndham 13 G3
Yadua 14 A2
Yagasa Cluster 14 B3
Yandé, Î. 14 T17
Yandina 14 M10
Yanuca 14 B1
Yaqaga 14 A2
Yasawa 14 A1
Yasawa Group 14 A1
Yaté 14 V26
Yates Pt. 13 E2
Young Ra. 13 E4

NAMES OF IMPORTANT TOWNS AND PHYSICAL FEATURES *

English to reo Māori and reo Māori to English

English	*reo Māori*
Ashburton	Hakatere
Auckland	Tāmaki-makau-rau
Blenheim	Te Waiharakeke
Cambridge	Kemureti
Chatham Islands	Wharekauri
Christchurch	Ōtautahi
Cook, Mt	Maunga Aoraki
D'Urville Island	Rangitoto ki te tonga
Dunedin	Ōtepoti
Gisborne	Tūranga-nui-a-Kiwa
Hamilton	Kirikiriroa
Hastings	Heretaunga
Hāwera	Te Hāwera
Invercargill	Waihōpai
Masterton	Whakaoriori
Napier	Ahuriri
Nelson	Wakatū
New Plymouth	Ngāmotu
New Zealand	Aotearoa
North Island	Te Ika-a-Māui
Palmerston North	Te Papa-i-oea
Queenstown	Tahuna
Rolleston	Roretana or Tauwharekākaho
South Island	Te Waipounamu
Southern Alps	Tiritiri o te Moana
Stewart Island	Rakiura
Taupo	Taupō-nui-a-Tia
Tauranga	Tauranga-moana
Timaru	Te Tihi-o-Maru
Upper Hutt	Orongomai
Wanganui	Whanganui
Wellington	Te Whanga-nui-a-Tara
White Island	Whakaari

reo Māori	*English*
Ahuriri	Napier
Aotearoa	New Zealand
Hakatere	Ashburton
Heretaunga	Hastings
Kemureti	Cambridge
Kirikiriroa	Hamilton
Maunga Aoraki	Cook, Mt
Ngāmotu	New Plymouth
Orongomai	Upper Hutt
Ōtautahi	Christchurch
Ōtepoti	Dunedin
Rakiura	Stewart Island
Rangitoto ki te tonga	D'Urville Island
Roretana or Tauwharekākaho	Rolleston
Tahuna	Queenstown
Tāmaki-makau-rau	Auckland
Taupō-nui-a-Tia	Taupo
Tauranga-moana	Tauranga
Te Hāwera	Hāwera
Te Ika-a-Māui	North Island
Te Papa-i-oea	Palmerston North
Te Tihi-o-Maru	Timaru
Te Waiharakeke	Blenheim
Te Waipounamu	South Island
Te Whanga-nui-a-Tara	Wellington
Tiritiri o te Moana	Southern Alps
Tūranga-nui-a-Kiwa	Gisborne
Waihōpai	Invercargill
Wakatū	Nelson
Whakaari	White Island
Whakaoriori	Masterton
Whanganui	Wanganui
Wharekauri	Chatham Islands

*Towns with the largest populations included. Placenames without an English language alternative are not shown.

THE WORLD

NGĀ TŌPITO O TE AO	COMPASS POINTS
Raki	North
Tonga	South
Rāwhiti	East
Hauāuru	West
Te Tai Tokerau	Northern Area
Te Tai Tonga	Southern Area
Te Tai Rāwhiti	Eastern Area
Te Tai Hauāuru	Western Area

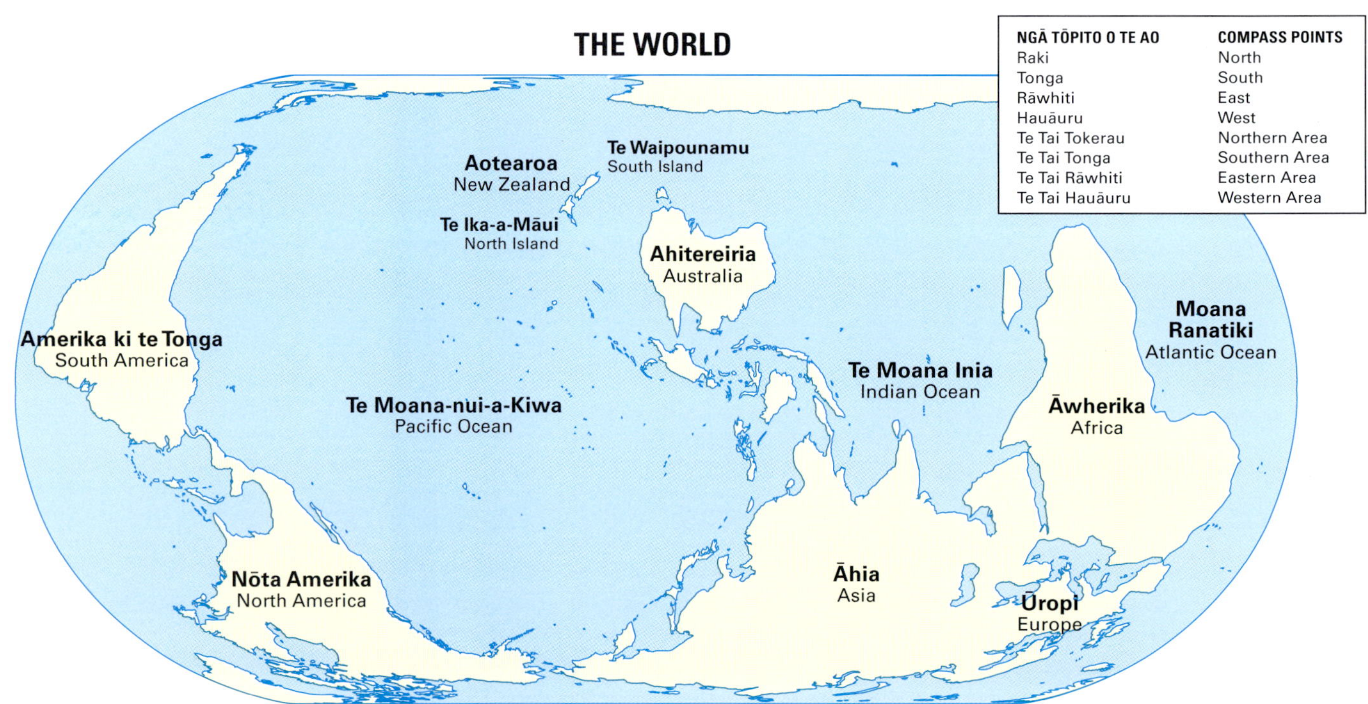

WORLD MAPS

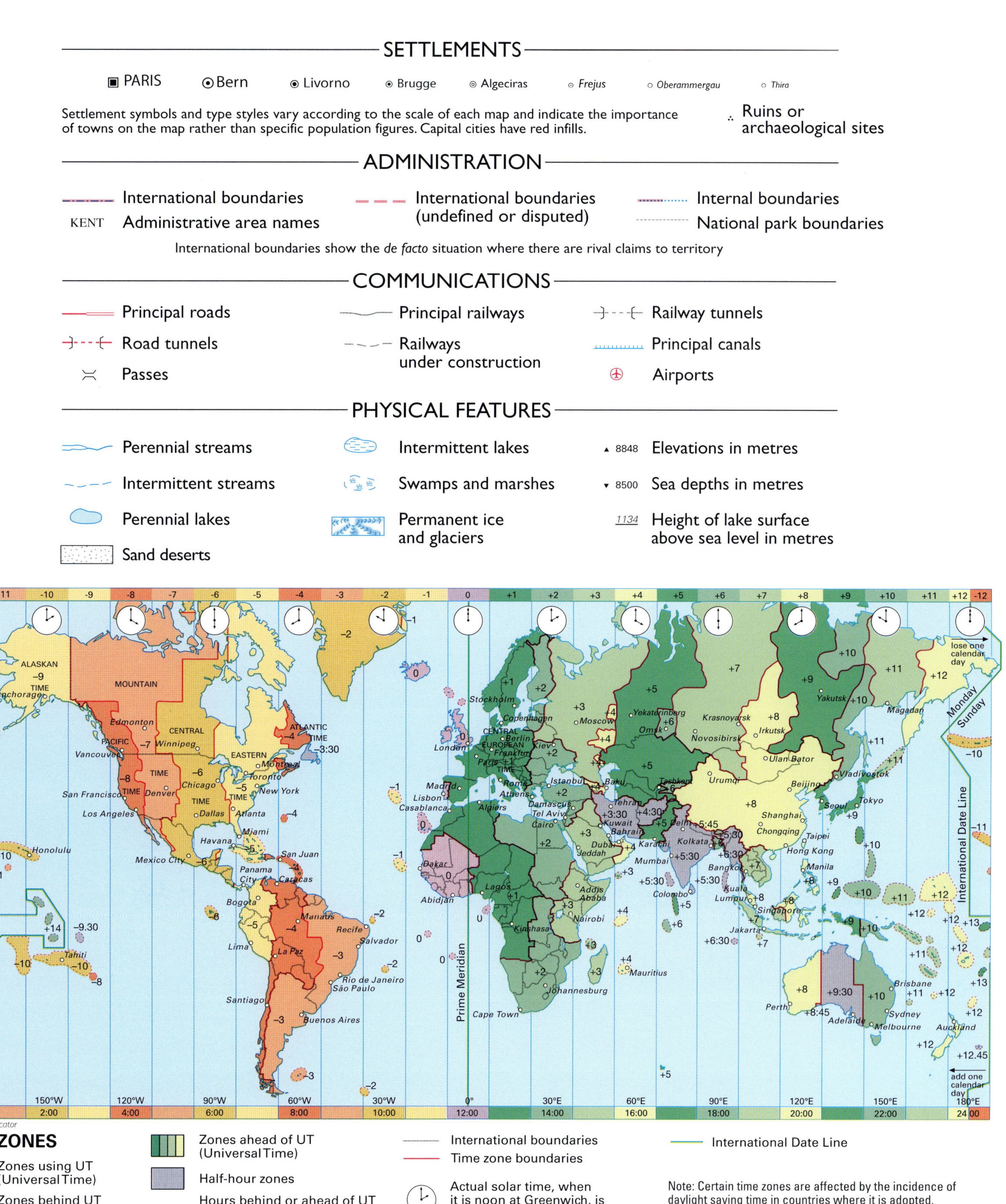

SETTLEMENTS
PARIS
Bern
Livorno
Brugge
Algeciras
Frejus
Oberammergau
Thira
Settlement symbols and type styles vary according to the scale of each map and indicate the importance of towns on the map rather than specific population figures. Capital cities have red infills.
Ruins or archaeological sites
ADMINISTRATION
International boundaries
International boundaries (undefined or disputed)
Internal boundaries
KENT
Administrative area names
National park boundaries
International boundaries show the de facto situation where there are rival claims to territory
COMMUNICATIONS
Principal roads
Principal railways
Railway tunnels
Road tunnels
Railways under construction
Principal canals
Passes
Airports
PHYSICAL FEATURES
Perennial streams
Intermittent lakes
8848
Elevations in metres
Intermittent streams
Swamps and marshes
8500
Sea depths in metres
Perennial lakes
Permanent ice and glaciers
1134
Height of lake surface above sea level in metres
Sand deserts
Projection: Mercator
TIME ZONES
Zones using UT (Universal Time)
Zones behind UT (Universal Time)
Zones ahead of UT (Universal Time)
Half-hour zones
10
Hours behind or ahead of UT (Universal Time)
International boundaries
Time zone boundaries
Actual solar time, when it is noon at Greenwich, is shown at the top of the map.
International Date Line
Note: Certain time zones are affected by the incidence of daylight saving time in countries where it is adopted.
UT (Universal Time) has replaced GMT (Greenwich Mean Time).
International Date Line
Prime Meridian
lose one calendar day
add one calendar day
Monday
Sunday
180°W
150°W
120°W
90°W
60°W
30°W
0°
30°E
60°E
90°E
120°E
150°E
180°E
24:00
2:00
4:00
6:00
8:00
10:00
12:00
14:00
16:00
18:00
20:00
22:00
ALASKAN TIME
MOUNTAIN TIME
PACIFIC TIME
CENTRAL TIME
EASTERN TIME
ATLANTIC TIME
CENTRAL EUROPEAN TIME
Anchorage
Edmonton
Winnipeg
Vancouver
Montreal
Toronto
New York
Chicago
Denver
San Francisco
Los Angeles
Dallas
Atlanta
Miami
Havana
Mexico City
Honolulu
San Juan
Panama City
Caracas
Bogota
Manaus
Recife
Salvador
Lima
La Paz
Rio de Janeiro
São Paulo
Santiago
Buenos Aires
Tahiti
Auckland
Stockholm
Copenhagen
Moscow
London
Berlin
Frankfurt
Paris
Kiev
Madrid
Lisbon
Casablanca
Rome
Athens
Istanbul
Algiers
Damascus
Tel Aviv
Cairo
Dakar
Lagos
Abidjan
Kinshasa
Nairobi
Addis Ababa
Johannesburg
Cape Town
Mauritius
Baku
Tehran
Kuwait
Bahrain
Dubai
Jeddah
Karachi
Delhi
Mumbai
Kolkata
Colombo
Tashkent
Yekaterinburg
Omsk
Novosibirsk
Krasnoyarsk
Irkutsk
Yakutsk
Magadan
Ulan Bator
Urumqi
Beijing
Vladivostok
Seoul
Tokyo
Shanghai
Chongqing
Taipei
Hong Kong
Manila
Bangkok
Kuala Lumpur
Singapore
Jakarta
Perth
Adelaide
Brisbane
Sydney
Melbourne
Auckland

THE WORLD : Physical

Equatorial Scale 1:95 000 000

PHYSICAL COMPARISONS

Continent	Area, '000 km	Coldest place, °C		Hottest place, °C		Wettest place (average annual rainfall, mm)		Driest place (average annual rainfall, mm)
Asia	44,500	Oymyakon, Russia -70˚C	1	Tirat Zevi, Israel 54˚C	8	Mawsynram, India 11,870	15	Aden, Yemen 46
Africa	30,302	Ifrane, Morocco -24˚C	2	Kebili, Tunisia 55˚C	9	Debundscha, Cameroon 10,290	16	Wadi Haifa, Sudan 2
North America	24,241	Snag, Yukon -63˚C	3	Death Valley, California 57˚C	10	Henderson Lake, Canada 6,500	17	Bataques, Mexico 30
South America	17,793	Sarmiento, Argentina -33˚C	4	Rivadavia, Argentina 49˚C	11	Quibdó, Colombia 8,990	18	Quillagua, Chile 0.6
Antarctica	14,000	Vostok -89˚C	5	Vanda Station 15˚C	12			
Europe	9,957	Ust'Shchugor, Russia -55˚C	6	Seville, Spain 50˚C	13	Crkvice, Montenegro 4,650	19	Astrakhan, Russia 160
Oceania	8,557	Charlotte Pass, Australia -22˚C	7	Oodnadatta, Australia 51˚C	14	Tully, Australia 4,550	20	Mulka, Australia 100

d - largest seas, '000 km²		World - largest lakes, '000 km²		World - longest rivers, km		World - largest islands, '000 km²		World - highest peaks, m		World - deepest trenches, m	
c Ocean 165,721	27	Caspian Sea 424	37	Nile 6,695	47	Greenland 2,176	57	Himalayas: Mt. Everest 8,849	67	Mariana Trench 11,022	77
tic Ocean 81,660	28	Lake Superior 82	38	Amazon 6,450	48	New Guinea 821	58	Karakoram Ra: K2 8,611	68	Tonga Trench 10,822	78
n Ocean 73,442	29	Lake Victoria 69	39	Yangtze 6,380	49	Borneo 741	59	Pamirs: Ismail Samani Pk. 7,495	69	Japan Trench 10,554	79
: Ocean 14,351	30	Lake Huron 60	40	Mississippi-Missouri 5,971	50	Madagascar 587	60	Tian Shan: Pik Pobedy 7,439	70	Kuril Trench 10,542	80
erranean Sea 2,966	31	Lake Michigan 58	41	Yenisey-Angara 5,550	51	Baffin Island 508	61	Andes: Aconcagua 6,962	71	Mindanao Trench 10,497	81
China Sea 2,318	32	Lake Tanganyika 33	42	Hwang-Ho 5,464	52	Sumatra 474	62	Rocky Mts: Denali 6,190	72	Kermadec Trench 10,047	82
g Sea 2,274	33	Lake Baikal 31	43	Ob-Irtysh 5,410	53	Honshu 231	63	East Africa: Mt. Kilimanjaro 5,895	73	Bougainville Trench 9,140	83
bean Sea 1,942	34	Great Bear Lake 31	44	Congo 4,670	54	Great Britain 230	64	Caucasus: Elbrus 5,642	74	Milwaukee Deep 8,605	84
of Mexico 1,813	35	Lake Malawi 31	45	Mekong 4,500	55	Victoria Island 212	65	Antarctica: Vinson Massif 4,897	75	South Sandwich Island Trench 8,428	85
f Okhotsk 1,528	36	Great Slave Lake 29	46	Amur 4,400	56	Ellesmere Island 197	66	Alps: Mt. Blanc 4,808	76	Aleutian Trench 7,822	86

Equatorial Scale 1:95 000 000

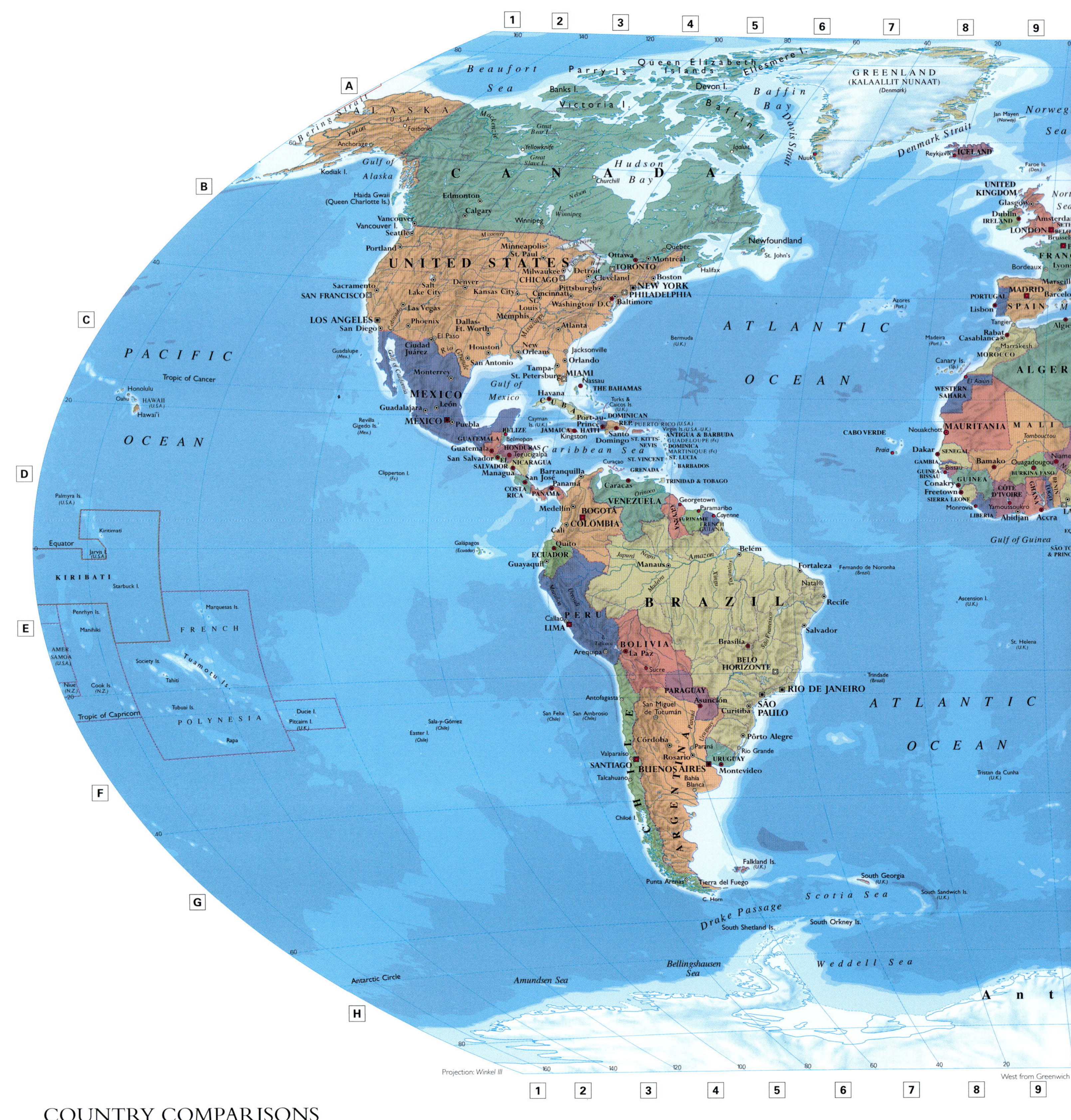

COUNTRY COMPARISONS

Country	Population in thousands 2024 estimate	Area '000 km²	Country	Population in thousands 2024 estimate	Area '000 km²	Country	Population in thousands 2024 estimate	Area '000 km²	Country	Population in thousands 2024 estimate	Area '000 km²	Country	Population in thousands 2024 estimate
China	1,416,043	9,597	Japan	123,202	378	United Kingdom	68,459	242	Uganda	49,283	241	Saudi Arabia	36,544
India	1,409,128	3,287	Ethiopia	118,550	1,104	France	68,375	552	Spain	47,280	498	Uzbekistan	36,521
United States	341,963	9,629	Philippines	118,277	300	Tanzania	67,462	945	Algeria	47,022	2,382	Ukraine	35,662
Indonesia	281,562	1,905	Congo, Dem. Rep.	115,403	2,345	Italy	60,965	301	Argentina	46,994	2,780	Ghana	34,589
Pakistan	252,364	796	Egypt	111,247	1,001	South Africa	60,443	1,221	Iraq	42,083	438	Malaysia	34,565
Nigeria	236,747	924	Vietnam	105,759	332	Kenya	58,246	580	Afghanistan	40,122	652	Mozambique	33,351
Brazil	220,052	8,514	Iran	88,387	1,648	Myanmar	57,527	677	Canada	38,795	9,971	Peru	32,600
Bangladesh	168,697	144	Turkey	84,120	775	South Korea	52,082	99	Poland	38,746	323	Yemen	32,140
Russia	140,821	17,075	Germany	84,119	357	Sudan	50,467	1,886	Morocco	37,388	447	Venezuela	31,250
Mexico	130,740	1,958	Thailand	69,921	513	Colombia	49,588	1,139	Angola	37,202	1,247	Nepal	31,122

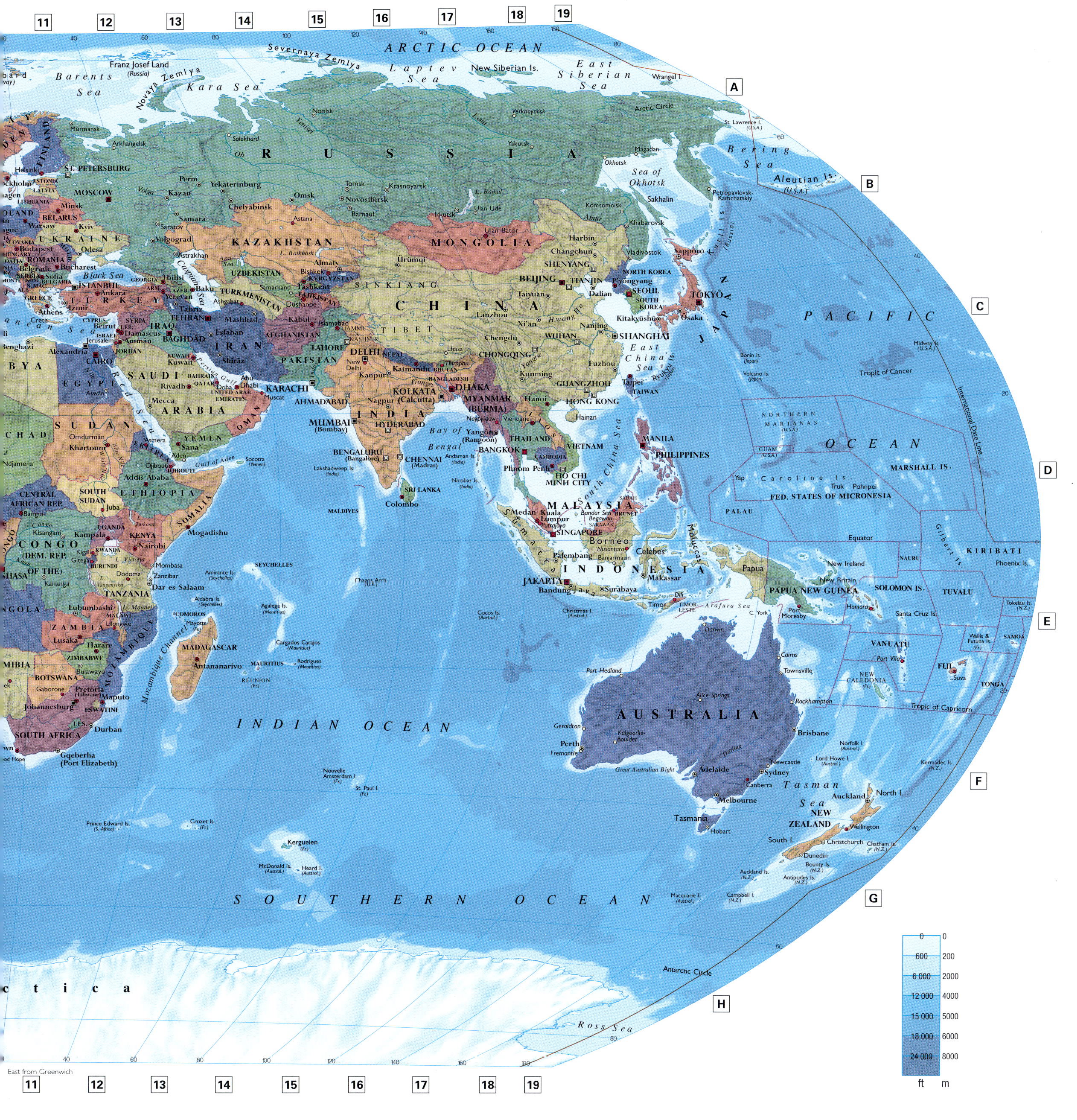

ry	Population in thousands 2024 estimate	Area '000 km²	Country	Population in thousands 2024 estimate	Area '000 km²	Country	Population in thousands 2024 estimate	Area '000 km²	Country	Population in thousands 2024 estimate	Area '000 km²	Country	Population in thousands 2024 estimate	Area '000 km²
oon	30,966	475	Sri Lanka	21,983	66	Netherlands	17,772	42	Tunisia	12,049	164	Tajikistan	10,394	143
'Ivoire	29,982	322	Malawi	21,763	118	Zimbabwe	17,150	391	Belgium	11,978	31	Portugal	10,207	89
gascar	29,453	587	Zambia	20,799	753	Cambodia	17,064	181	Haiti	11,754	28	P.N.G.	10,046	463
lia	26,769	7,741	Kazakhstan	20,260	2,725	Benin	14,697	113	Jordan	11,174	89	U.A.E.	10,032	84
	26,343	1,267	Chad	19,094	1,284	Guinea	13,986	246	Cuba	10,966	111	Hungary	9,856	93
Korea	26,299	121	Senegal	18,848	197	Rwanda	13,623	26	Czechia	10,838	79	Honduras	9,529	112
	23,865	185	Chile	18,665	757	Burundi	13,590	28	Dominican Rep.	10,816	49	Belarus	9,501	208
n	23,595	36	Ecuador	18,310	284	Somalia	13,017	638	Azerbaijan	10,650	87	Israel	9,403	21
a Faso	23,042	274	Guatemala	18,255	109	South Sudan	12,704	620	Sweden	10,590	450	Sierra Leone	9,121	72
	21,991	1,240	Romania	18,148	238	Bolivia	12,312	1,099	Greece	10,461	132	Austria	8,968	84

6 POLAR REGIONS

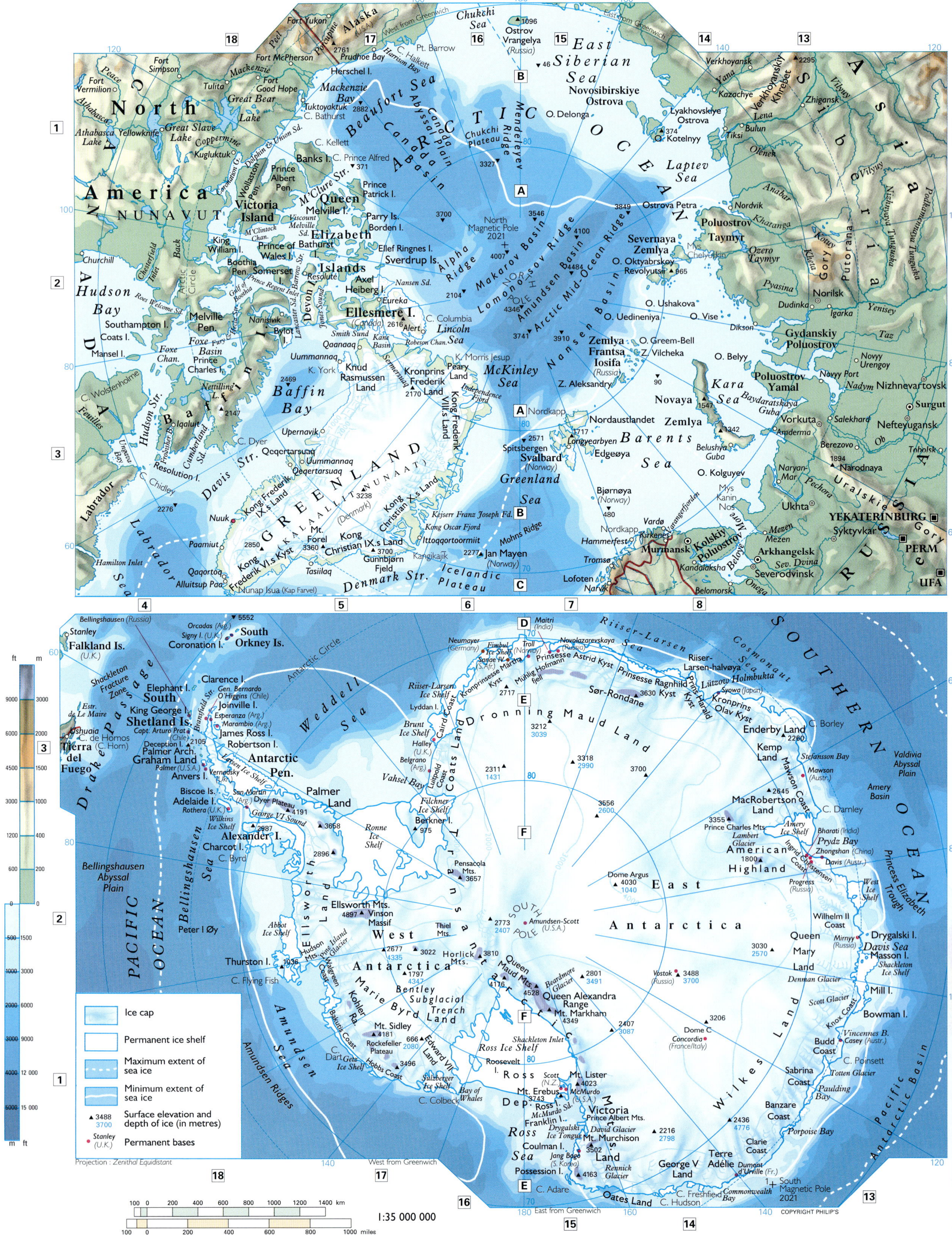

1:10 000 000

ICELAND
on same scale
West from Greenwich
East from Greenwich
NORWEGIAN SEA
BARENTS SEA
NORWAY
SWEDEN
FINLAND
Lappland
Norrland
Svealand
Götaland
Gulf of Bothnia
Gulf of Finland
Gulf of Riga
BALTIC SEA
Skagerrak
Kattegat
DENMARK
ESTONIA
LATVIA
LITHUANIA
BELARUS
RUSSIA
POLAND
GERMANY
CZECHIA
UKRAINE
KARELIA
Kolskiy Poluostrov
Beloye More (White Sea)
Ladozhskoye Ozero
Onezhskoye Ozero
OSLO
STOCKHOLM
HELSINKI
Tallinn
Riga
Vilnius
MINSK
KØBENHAVN (Copenhagen)
WARSZAWA (Warsaw)
BERLIN
PRAHA (Prague)
MOSKVA (Moscow)
KYIV (Kiev)
SANKT-PETERBURG
Reykjavík
Projection: Conical with two standard parallels
COPYRIGHT PHILIP'S
m ft

ENGLAND AND WALES

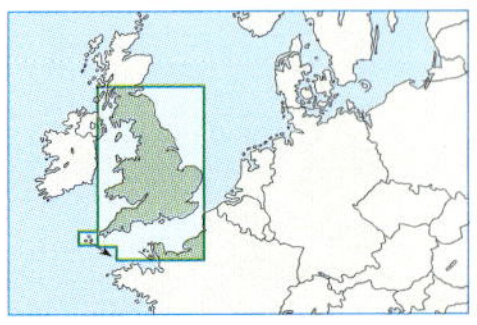

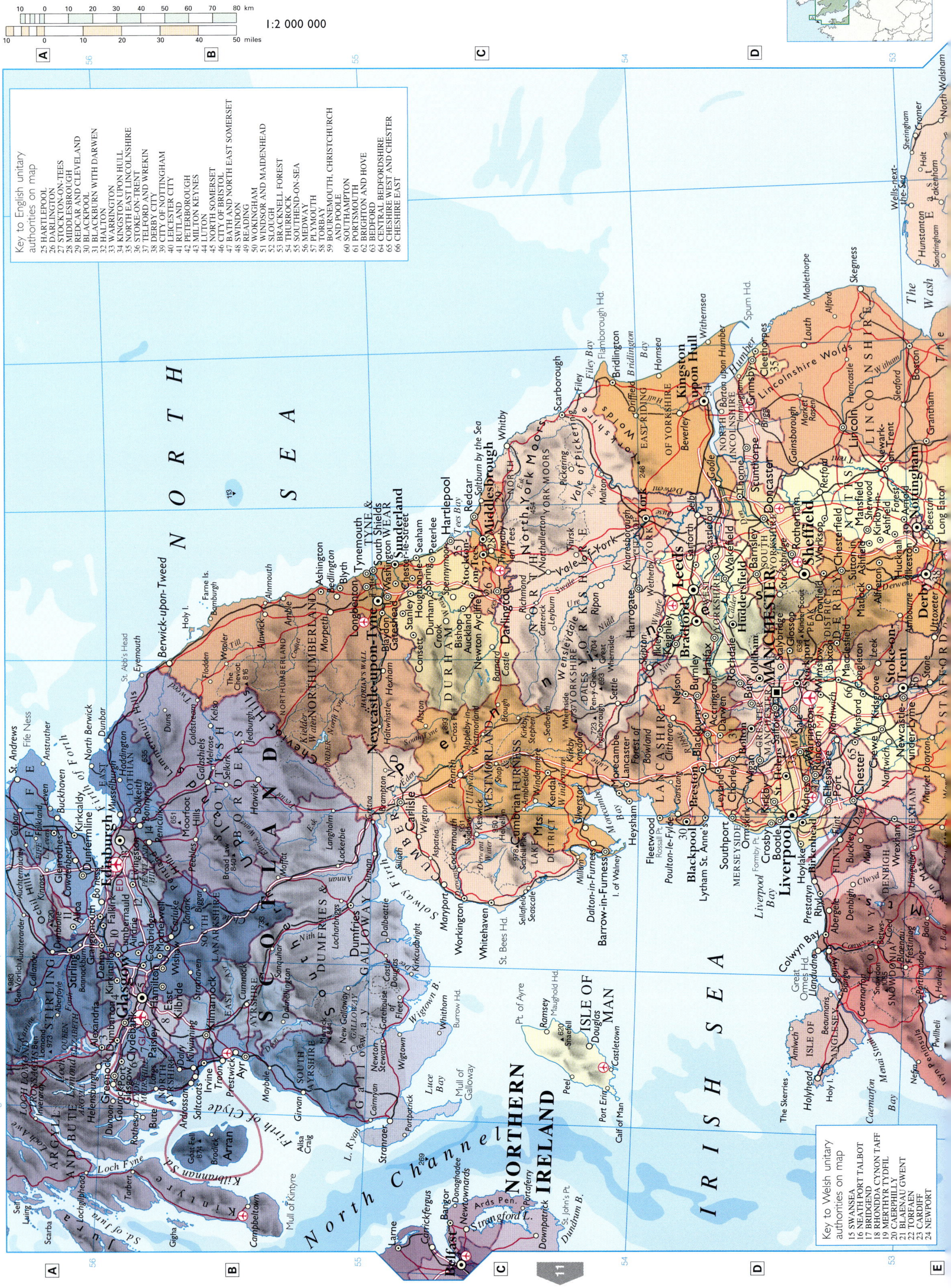
10 0 10 20 30 40 50 60 70 80 km
10 0 10 20 30 40 50 miles
1:2 000 000
Key to English unitary authorities on map
25 HARTLEPOOL
26 DARLINGTON
27 STOCKTON-ON-TEES
28 MIDDLESBROUGH
29 REDCAR AND CLEVELAND
30 BLACKPOOL
31 BLACKBURN WITH DARWEN
32 HALTON
33 WARRINGTON
34 KINGSTON UPON HULL
35 NORTH EAST LINCOLNSHIRE
36 STOKE-ON-TRENT
37 TELFORD AND WREKIN
38 DERBY CITY
39 CITY OF NOTTINGHAM
40 LEICESTER CITY
41 RUTLAND
42 PETERBOROUGH
43 MILTON KEYNES
44 LUTON
45 NORTH SOMERSET
46 CITY OF BRISTOL
47 BATH AND NORTH EAST SOMERSET
48 SWINDON
49 READING
50 WOKINGHAM
51 WINDSOR AND MAIDENHEAD
52 SLOUGH
53 BRACKNELL FOREST
54 THURROCK
55 SOUTHEND-ON-SEA
56 MEDWAY
57 PLYMOUTH
58 TORBAY
59 BOURNEMOUTH, CHRISTCHURCH AND POOLE
60 SOUTHAMPTON
61 PORTSMOUTH
62 BRIGHTON AND HOVE
63 BEDFORD
64 CENTRAL BEDFORDSHIRE
65 CHESHIRE WEST AND CHESTER
66 CHESHIRE EAST
Key to Welsh unitary authorities on map
15 SWANSEA
16 NEATH PORT TALBOT
17 BRIDGEND
18 RHONDDA CYNON TAFF
19 MERTHYR TYDFIL
20 CAERPHILLY
21 BLAENAU GWENT
22 TORFAEN
23 CARDIFF
24 NEWPORT
NORTH SEA
IRISH SEA
SCOTLAND
NORTHERN IRELAND
ISLE OF MAN
North Channel

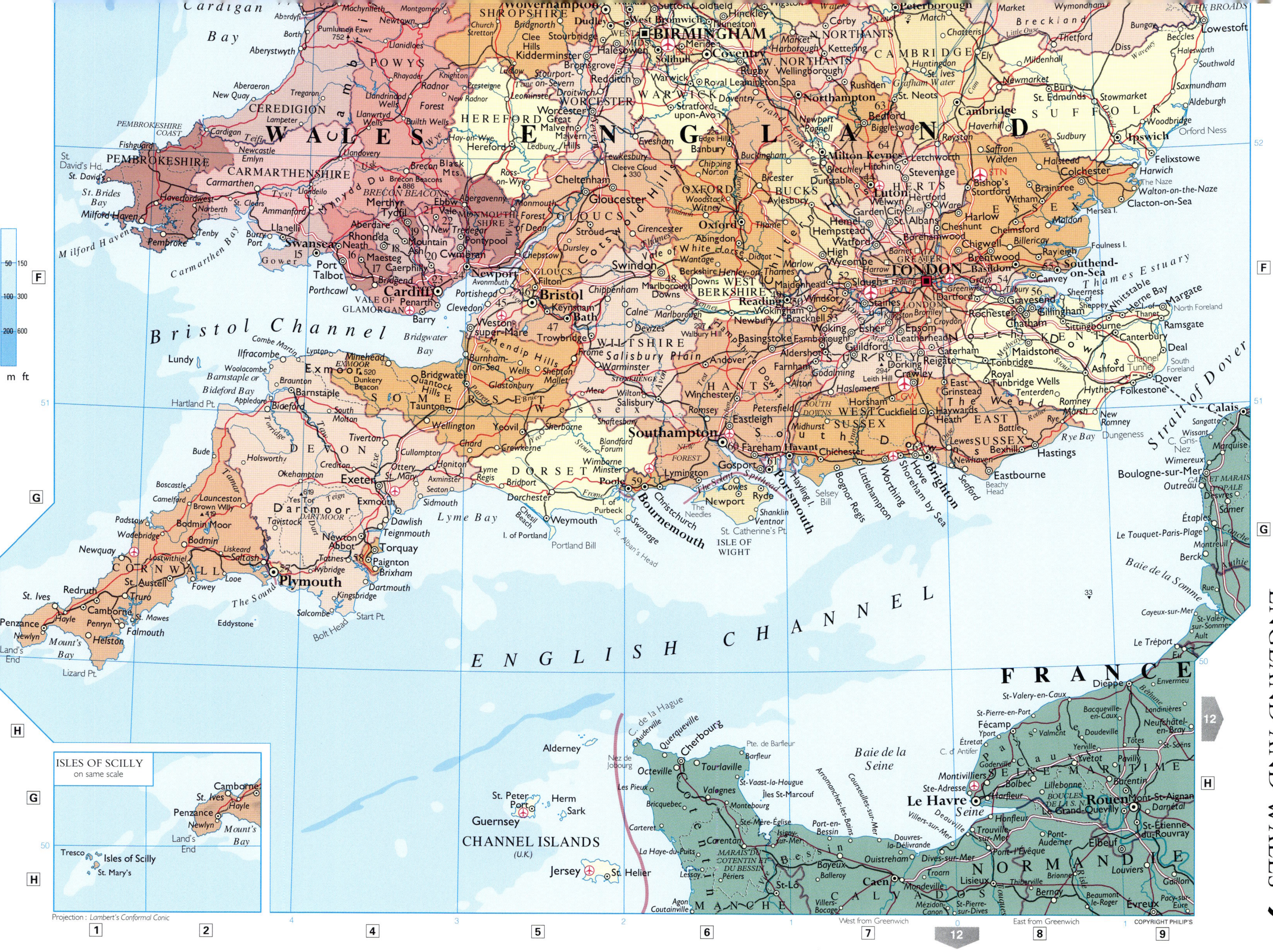

WALES
ENGLAND
FRANCE
ENGLISH CHANNEL
Bristol Channel
Strait of Dover
Thames Estuary
LONDON
BIRMINGHAM
Bristol
Cardiff
Swansea
Newport
Southampton
Portsmouth
Bournemouth
Brighton
Plymouth
Exeter
Oxford
Cambridge
Gloucester
Bath
Salisbury
Reading
Canterbury
Dover
Folkestone
Hastings
Eastbourne
Ipswich
Colchester
Chelmsford
Torquay
Weymouth
Dorchester
Taunton
Newquay
Penzance
Falmouth
Truro
ISLE OF WIGHT
CHANNEL ISLANDS (U.K.)
Guernsey
Jersey
Alderney
Sark
Herm
St. Helier
St. Peter Port
Cherbourg
Le Havre
Rouen
Caen
Dieppe
Calais
Boulogne-sur-Mer
Baie de la Seine
Baie de la Somme
NORMANDIE
Lyme Bay
Cardigan Bay
Carmarthen Bay
Dartmoor
Exmoor
Lundy
ISLES OF SCILLY on same scale
Isles of Scilly
St. Mary's
Tresco
Land's End
Lizard Pt.
Projection : Lambert's Conformal Conic
West from Greenwich
East from Greenwich
COPYRIGHT PHILIP'S
m
ft
50–150
100–300
200–600

1:2 000 000

km 10 0 10 20 30 40 50 60 70 80

miles 10 0 10 20 30 40 50

Key to Scottish unitary authorities on map

1 ABERDEEN CITY
2 DUNDEE CITY
3 WEST DUNBARTONSHIRE
4 EAST DUNBARTONSHIRE
5 GLASGOW CITY
6 INVERCLYDE
7 RENFREWSHIRE
8 EAST RENFREWSHIRE
9 NORTH LANARKSHIRE
10 FALKIRK
11 CLACKMANNANSHIRE
12 WEST LOTHIAN
13 CITY OF EDINBURGH
14 MIDLOTHIAN

ORKNEY IS. on same scale

SHETLAND IS. on same scale

m ft: 0 · 50 150 · 100 300 · 200 600 · 500 1500 · 1000 3000

Projection: Lambert's Conformal Conic

West from Greenwich

11

8

1:2 000 000

Key to administrative areas in Northern Ireland
1 CAUSEWAY COAST AND GLENS
2 DERRY AND STRABANE
3 MID AND EAST ANTRIM
4 ANTRIM AND NEWTOWNABBEY
5 ARDS AND NORTH DOWN
6 BELFAST CITY
7 LISBURN AND CASTLEREAGH
8 ARMAGH, BANBRIDGE AND CRAIGAVON
9 NEWRY, MOURNE AND DOWN
ATLANTIC OCEAN
CELTIC SEA
IRISH SEA
St. George's Channel
North Channel
SCOTLAND
WALES
IRELAND
NORTHERN IRELAND
Ulster
Connaught
Leinster
Munster
DONEGAL
SLIGO
LEITRIM
MAYO
ROSCOMMON
LONGFORD
CAVAN
MONAGHAN
LOUTH
MEATH
WESTMEATH
GALWAY
OFFALY
KILDARE
DUBLIN
FINGAL
SOUTH DUBLIN
DÚN LAOGHAIRE-RATHDOWN
WICKLOW
LAOIS
CARLOW
KILKENNY
WEXFORD
WATERFORD
TIPPERARY
CLARE
LIMERICK
KERRY
CORK
Dublin
Belfast
Londonderry (Derry)
Cork
Limerick
Galway
Waterford
Sligo
Dundalk
Drogheda
Kilkenny
Tralee
Killarney
Wexford
Athlone
Ennis
Shannon
Carrauntoohill 1041
Macgillycuddy's Reeks
Lough Neagh
Lough Corrib
Lough Derg
Lough Ree
Lower L. Erne
Upper Erne
Aran Is.
Galway Bay
Dingle Bay
Bantry Bay
Dublin Bay
Projection: Lambert's Conformal Conic
West from Greenwich
COPYRIGHT PHILIP'S
m ft

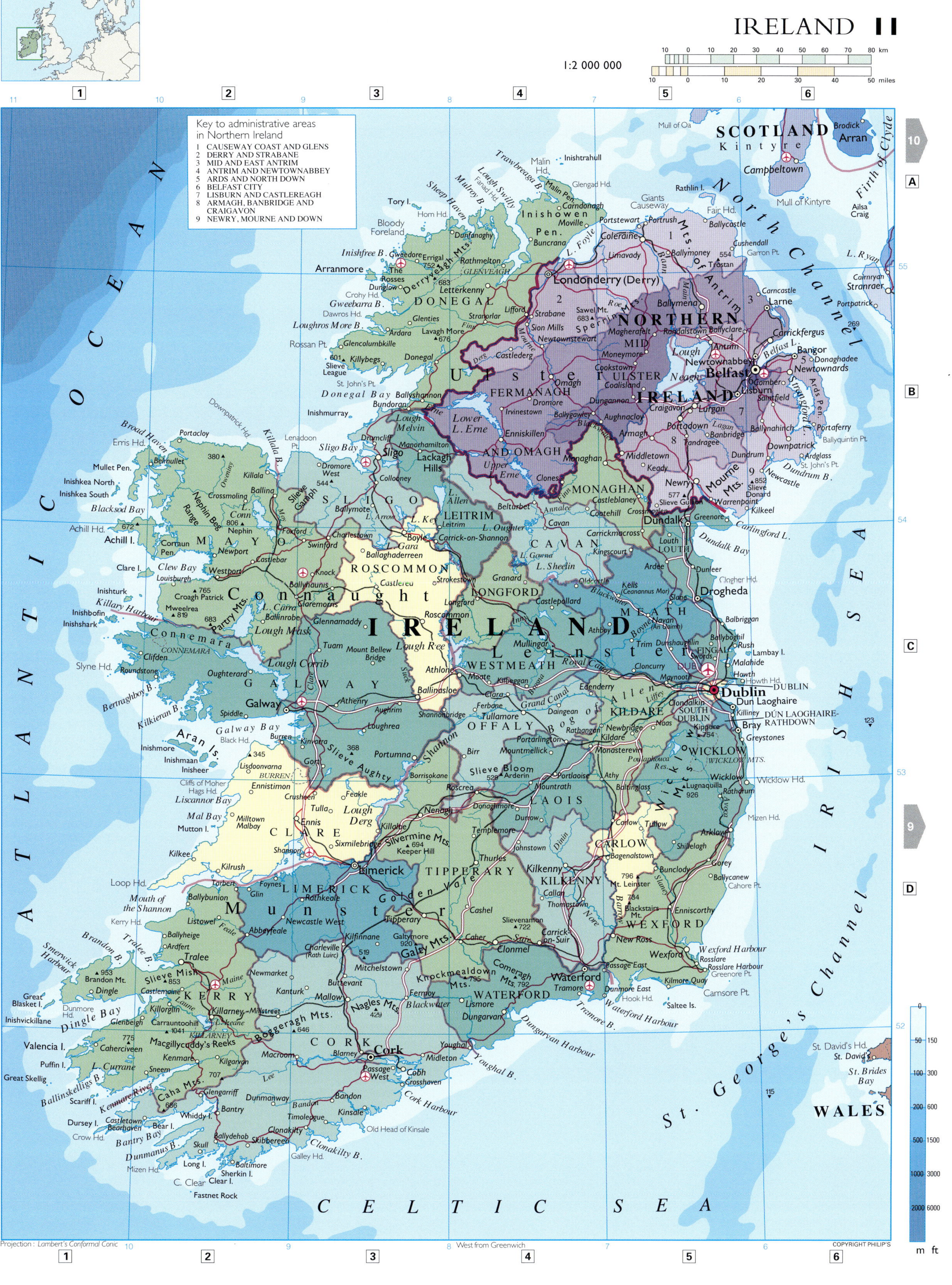

FRANCE

1:5 000 000

50 0 25 50 75 100 125 150 175 km

50 0 25 50 75 100 125 miles

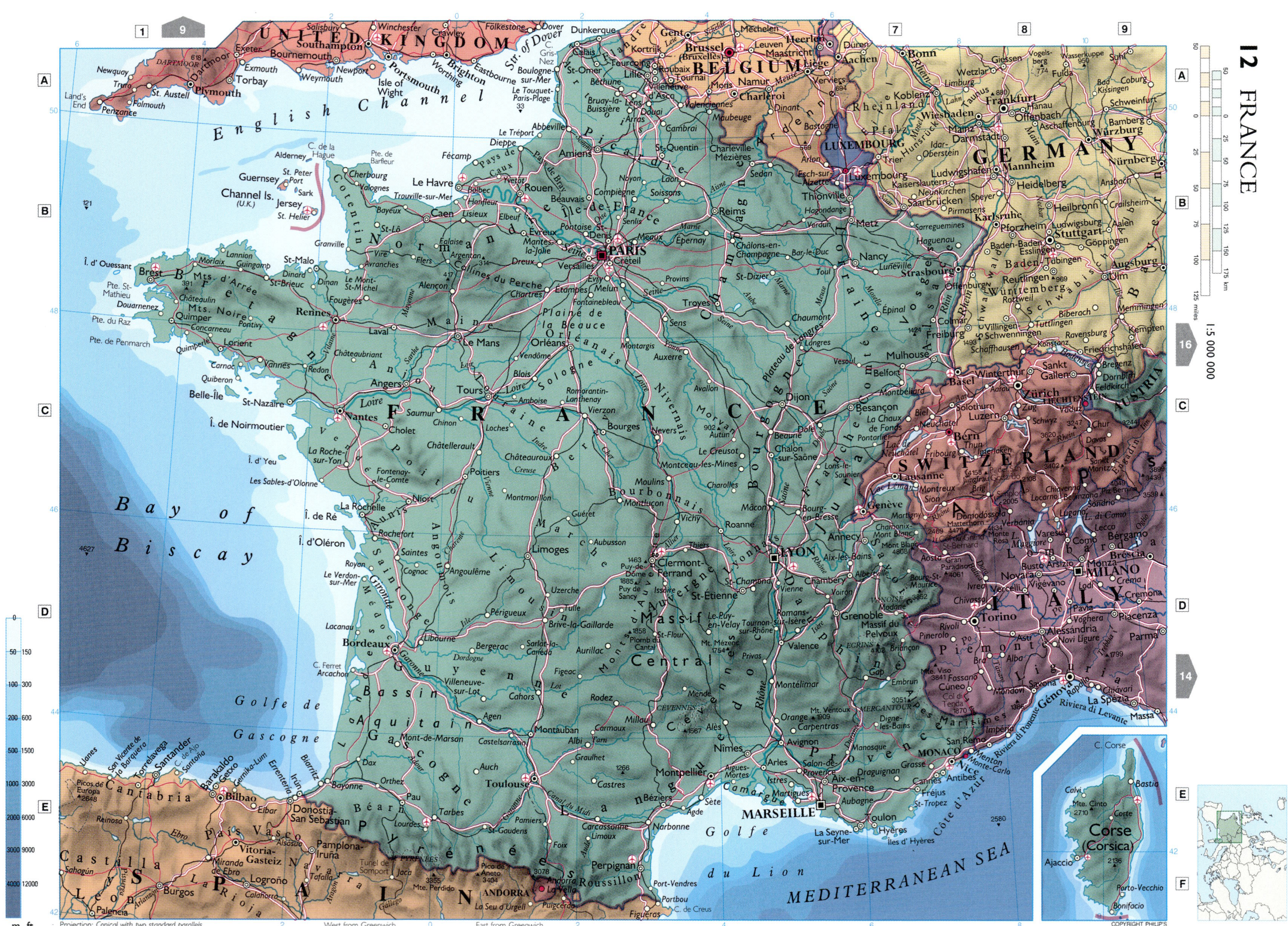

0 50 150 100 300 200 600 500 1500 1000 3000 2000 6000 3000 9000 4000 12000 m ft

1:5 000 000
50 0 25 50 75 100 125 150 175 km
50 0 25 50 75 100 125 miles
Projection: Conical with two standard parallels
COPYRIGHT PHILIPS
West from Greenwich
East from Greenwich
m ft
0
50 150
100 300
200 600
500 1500
1000 3000
2000 6000
3000 9000
4000 12000
MADRID
LISBOA
BARCELONA
Valencia
Sevilla
Zaragoza
Málaga
Alicante
Córdoba
Porto
Bilbao
Granada
Murcia
Valladolid
ALGER
Oran
Tanger
Menorca
Mallorca
Eivissa (Ibiza)
Formentera
Cabrera
Str. of Gibraltar
Gibraltar (U.K.)
Ceuta (Sp.)
Melilla (Sp.)
Alborán (Sp.)
ANDORRA
Golfe du Lion
G. de Cádiz
Golfo de Valencia
Costa Brava
Costa Dorada
Costa Blanca
Costa del Sol
Algarve
Mar Menor

SWITZERLAND
AUSTRIA
SLOVENIA
CROATIA
ITALIA
FRANCE
ALGERIA
TUNISIA
MALTA
SAN MARINO
MONACO
VATICANO
ADRIATIC SEA
LIGURIAN SEA
TYRRHENIAN SEA
MEDITE
Golfo di Génova
Golfo di Venézia
Corse (Corsica)
Sardegna (Sardinia)
Sicilia
Ìsole Eólie
Ìsole Égadi
Ìsole Pelagie (Italy)
Ìsole Ponziane
Pantelleria (Italy)
Ústica (Italy)
Bouches de Bonifacio
Str. di Messina
Golfe de Tunis
Golfe de Hammamet
Golfo dell' Asinara
G. di Oristano
G. di Cágliari
G. di Pálmas
ROMA
MILANO
Torino (Turin)
Génova
Venézia (Venice)
Firenze (Florence)
Nápoli
Palermo
Cágliari
Bologna
Trieste
Ljubljana
ZAGREB
TUNIS
Valletta
MARSEILLE
LYON
Grenoble
Nice
Toulon
Ajaccio
Bastia
Sássari
Messina
Réggio di Calábria
Catánia
Siracusa
Bari
Táranto
Foggia
Pescara
Ancona
Perúgia
Pisa
Livorno
Verona
Pádova
Trento
Bolzano
Udine
Rijeka
Split
Zadar
Constantine
Annaba
Skikda
Bizerte
Sousse
Kairouan
Monastir
Gozo
Rabat
Lampedusa
Linosa
Lampione
Elba
Capri
Íschia
Stromboli
Vesuvio
Etna
Mte. Cimone
Monti Nébrodi
Golfo di Génova
Riviera di Ponente
Riviera di Levante
Côte d'Azur
Provence
Dolomiti
Karnische Alpen
Karawanken
Istra
Krk
Cres
Lošinj
Pag
Dugi Otok
Hvar
Brač
Vis
Korčula
Palagruža (Cr.)
m ft

HUNGARY
ROMANIA
UKRAINE
SERBIA
BULGARIA
KOSOVO
MONTENEGRO
NORTH MACEDONIA
ALBANIA
GREECE
TURKEY
BLACK SEA
AEGEAN SEA
IONIAN SEA
MEDITERRANEAN SEA
Sea of Thrace
Sea of Crete
Mirtoo Sea
Marmara Denizi
Str. of Otranto
BUCUREŞTI (Bucharest)
BEOGRAD (Belgrade)
SOFIA
Sarajevo
Skopje
Tiranë
Podgorica
Pristina
ATHINA (Athens)
Thessaloniki (Salonica)
ISTANBUL
İZMIR (Smyrna)
BURSA
Constanţa
Varna
Burgas
Plovdiv
Crete
Rhodes
Lesbos
Limnos
Chios
Samos
Evia
Peloponnese
Kerkyra (Corfu)
Kefalonia (Cephalonia)
Zakynthos (Zante)
Northern Sporades
Cyclades
Dodecanese
Carpaţii Meridionali
Transilvania
Stara Planina
Rhodopi Planina
Pindos Oros
East from Greenwich
COPYRIGHT PHILIP'S

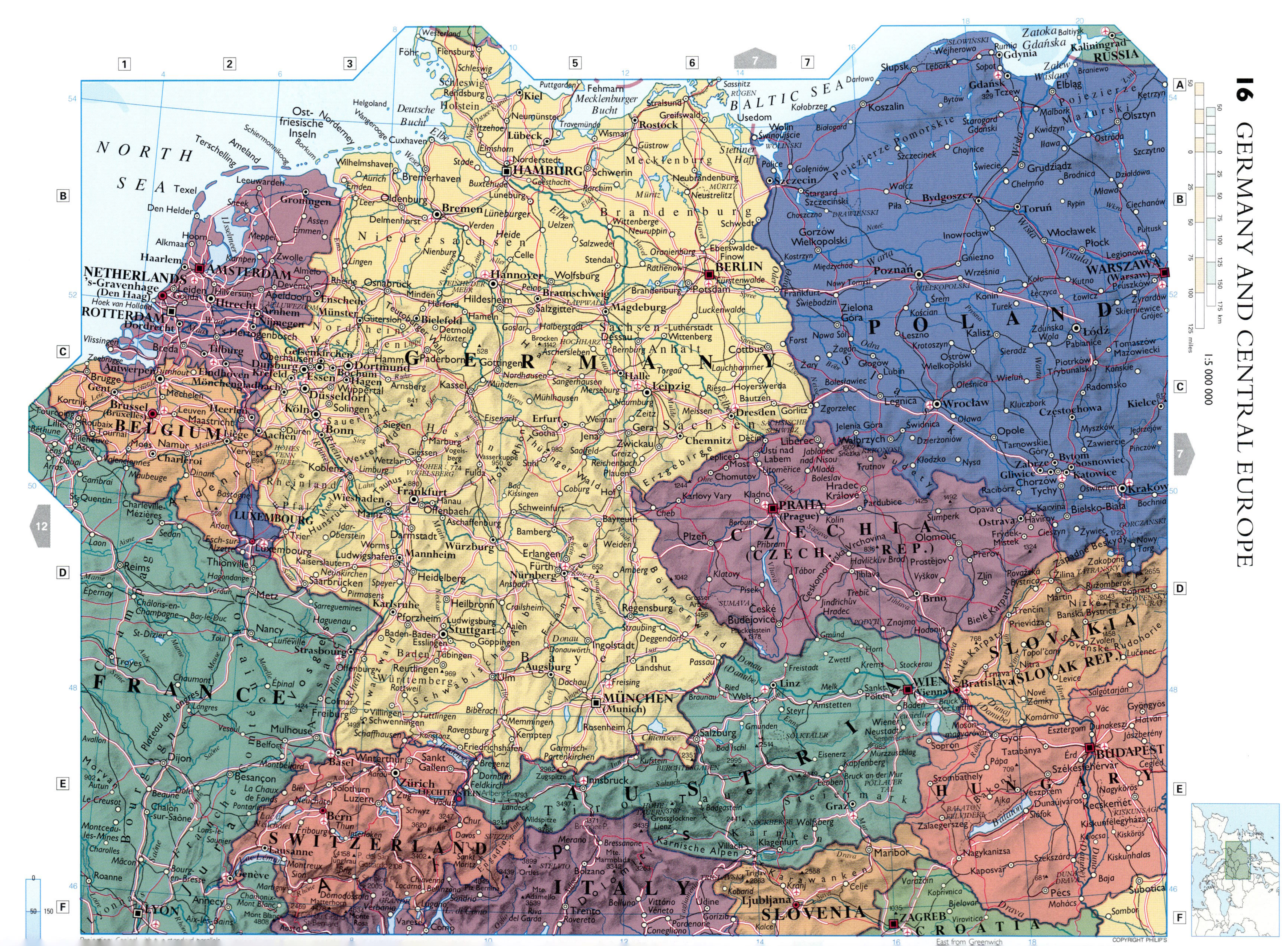

1:5 000 000
50 0 25 50 75 100 125 150 175 km
50 0 25 50 75 100 125 miles
NORTH SEA
BALTIC SEA
RUSSIA
POLAND
GERMANY
NETHERLANDS
BELGIUM
LUXEMBOURG
FRANCE
SWITZERLAND
AUSTRIA
ITALY
SLOVENIA
CROATIA
HUNGARY
SLOVAKIA (SLOVAK REP.)
CZECHIA (CZECH REP.)
BERLIN
WARSZAWA (Warsaw)
PRAHA (Prague)
WIEN (Vienna)
BUDAPEST
MÜNCHEN (Munich)
HAMBURG
AMSTERDAM
ZAGREB
East from Greenwich

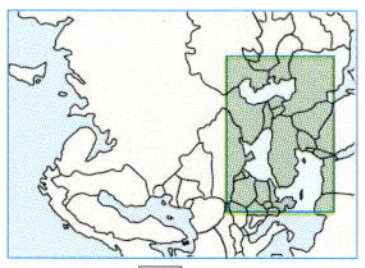

1:10 000 000

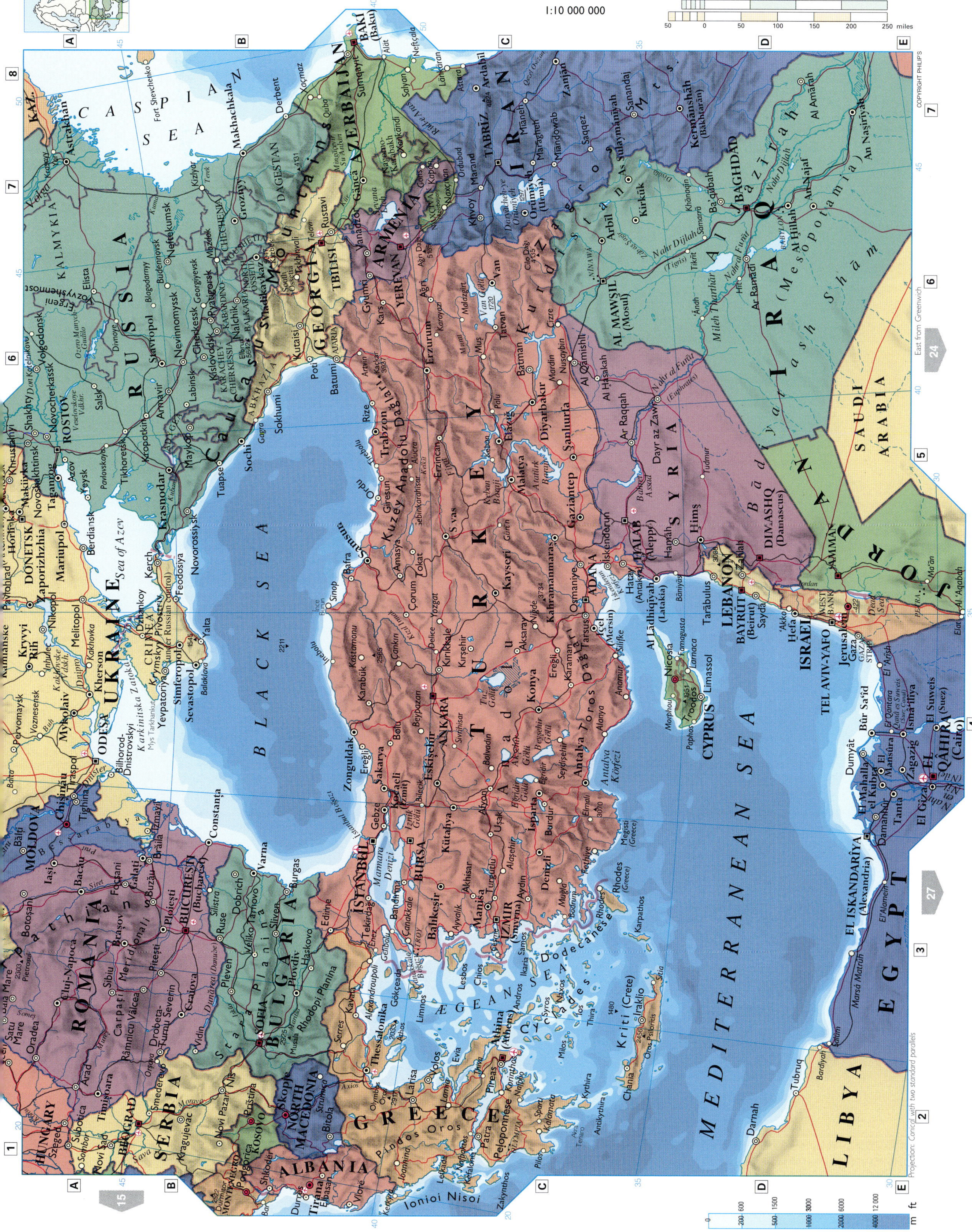

50 0 100 200 300 400 km

50 0 50 100 150 200 250 miles

Projection: Conical with two standard parallels

100 0 100 200 300 400 500 600 700 800 km
100 0 100 200 300 400 500 miles
1:20 000 000
RUSSIA
1 Adygea
2 Karachey-Cherkessia
3 Kabardino-Balkaria
4 North Ossetia
5 Ingushetia
6 Chechenia
7 Dagestan
8 Mordvinia
9 Chuvashia
10 Mari El
11 Tatarstan
12 Udmurtia
13 Khakassia
AZERBAIJAN
14 Naxçivan
GEORGIA
15 Ajaria
16 Abkhazia
UKRAINE
17 Crimea
Norwegian Sea
Barents Sea
Kara Sea
Gulf of Bothnia
Baltic Sea
Black Sea
Caspian Sea
Beloye More
NORWAY
SWEDEN
FINLAND
ESTONIA
LATVIA
LITHUANIA
BELARUS
POLAND
UKRAINE
GERMANY
DENMARK
GEORGIA
ARMENIA
AZERBAIJAN
TURKEY
IRAQ
IRAN
TURKMENISTAN
UZBEKISTAN
KAZAKHSTAN
KYRGYZSTAN
TAJIKISTAN
AFGHANISTAN
RUSSIA
OSLO
STOCKHOLM
HELSINKI
RIGA
MINSK
KYIV
MOSKVA
SANKT-PETERBURG
TBILISI
YEREVAN
BAKI (Baku)
TEHRAN
BAGHDAD
ASHGABAT
TOSHKENT
BISHKEK
ALMATY (Alma Ata)
Astana (Nur-Sultan)
Arkhangelsk
Murmansk
Nizhniy Novgorod
Kazan
Samara
Volgograd
Rostov
Astrakhan
Yekaterinburg
Chelyabinsk
Omsk
Novosibirsk
Barnaul
Perm
Ufa
Orenburg
Tyumen
Surgut
Vorkuta
Salekhard
Zemlya Frantsa Iosifa
Novaya Zemlya
Poluostrov Yamal
Ural
East from Greenwich
Projection: Conical Orthomorphic with two standard parallels

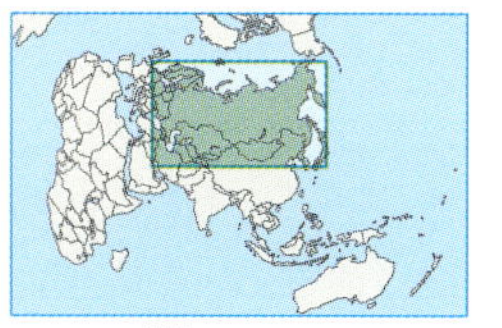

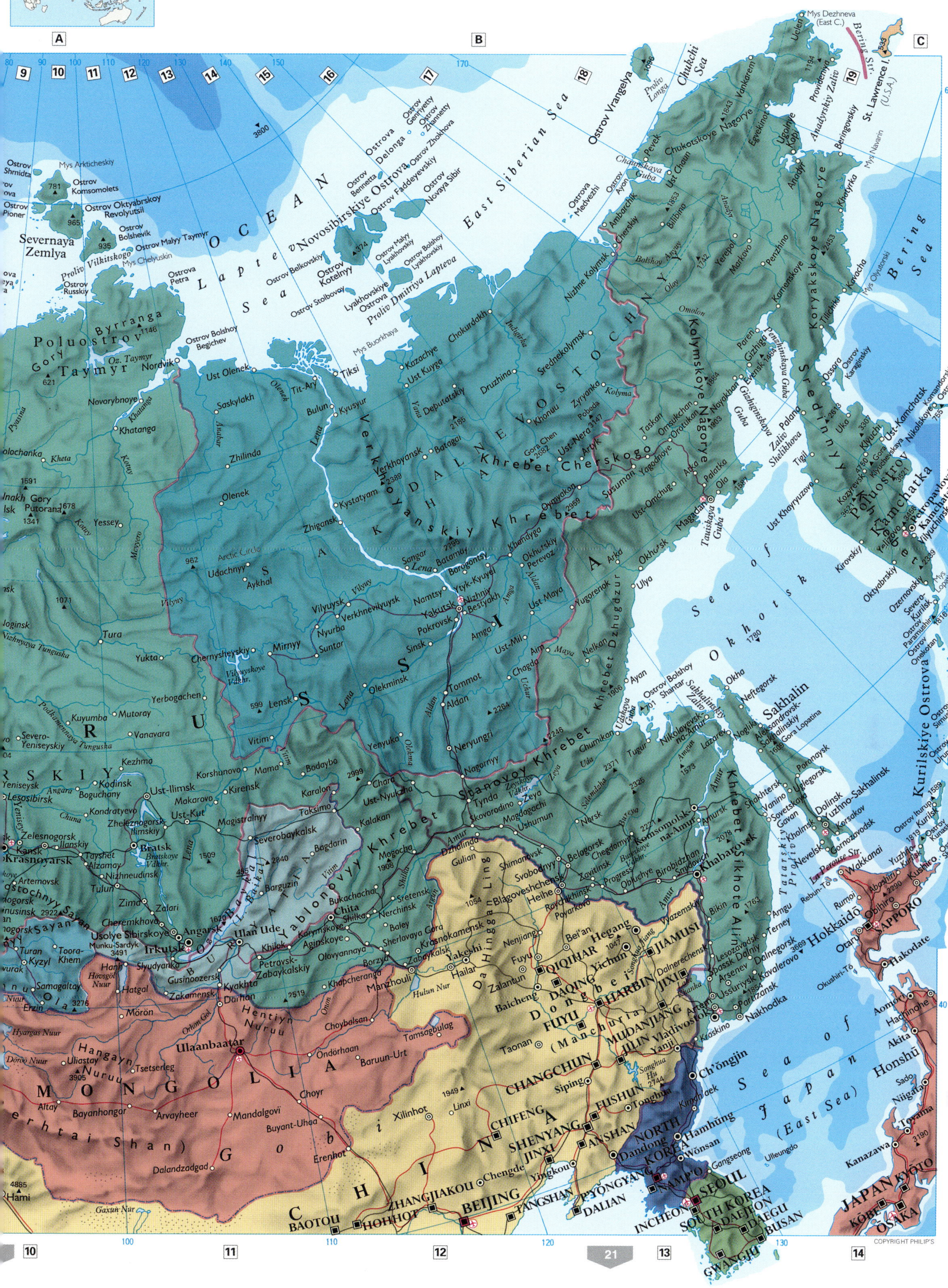

21

CHINA AND THE FAR EAST

1:15 000 000

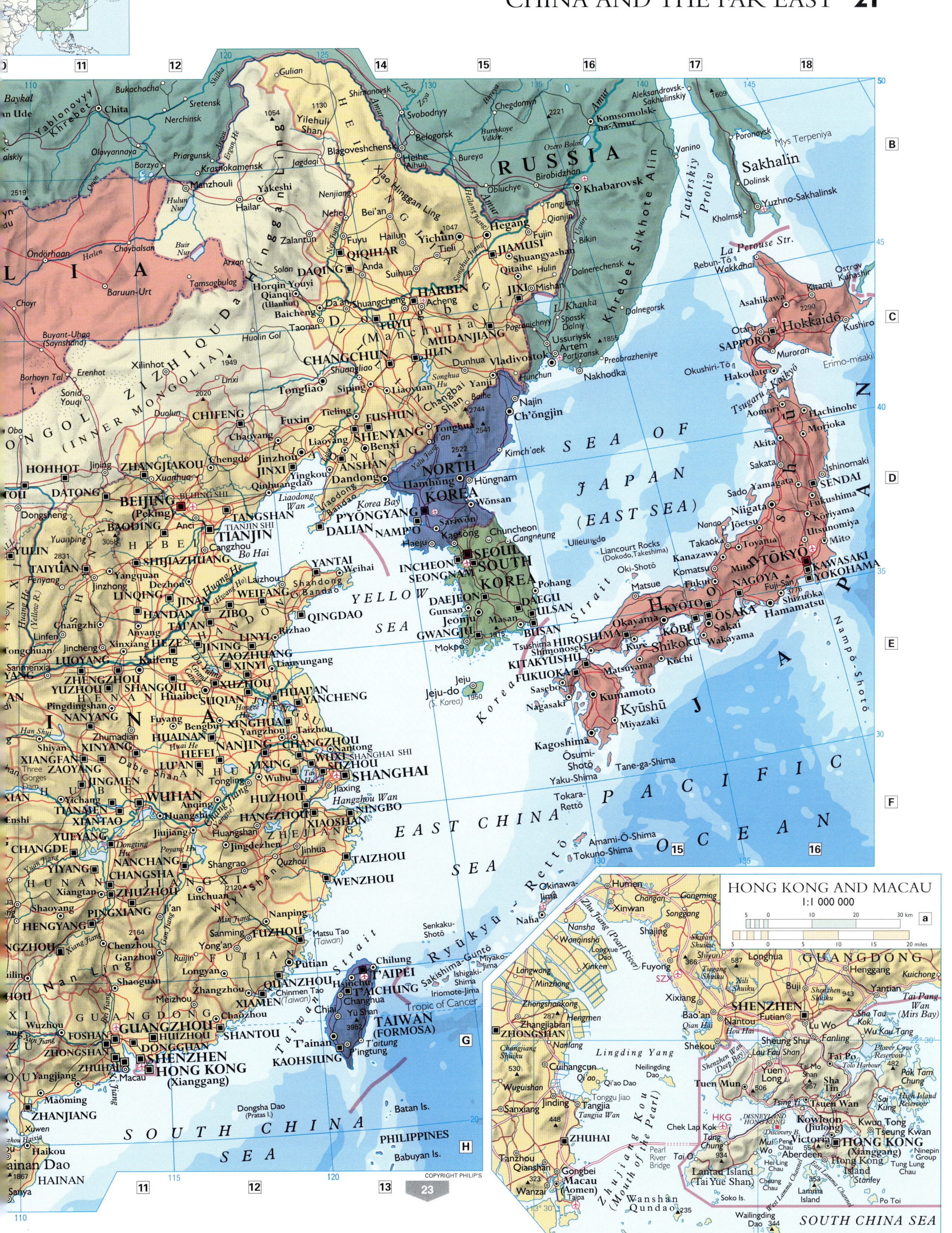
RUSSIA
Sakhalin
SEA OF JAPAN (EAST SEA)
YELLOW SEA
EAST CHINA SEA
SOUTH CHINA SEA
PACIFIC OCEAN
NORTH KOREA
SOUTH KOREA
TAIWAN (FORMOSA)
BEIJING (Peking)
TIANJIN
SHANGHAI
HONG KONG (Xianggang)
TOKYO
SEOUL
P'YŎNGYANG
TAIPEI
VLADIVOSTOK
HARBIN
Hokkaidō
Kyūshū
Shikoku
Tropic of Cancer
HONG KONG AND MACAU
1:1 000 000
SOUTH CHINA SEA
COPYRIGHT PHILIP'S

1:6 400 000

50 0 25 50 75 100 125 150 175 km
50 0 25 50 75 100 125 miles

CHINA
JIXI
Linkou
Novokachalinsk
L. Khanka
Kamen-Rybolov
Suifenhe
RUSSIA
Lesozavodsk
Rakitnoye
Kirovskiy
Ariadnoye
Gornyy
Spassk Dalniy
Yakovlevka
Lipovcy
Manzovka
Arseney
Ussuriysk
Artem
Trudovoye
Vladivostok
Nakhodka
Slavyanka
Zaliv Petra Velikogo
Hunchun
1498
Khasan
Najin
Ch'ŏngjin
NORTH KOREA
Sikhote Alin
Khrebet
1855
Lazo
Terney
Plastun
Dalnegorsk
Kavalerovo
Margaritovo
Preobrazheniye

SEA OF JAPAN (EAST SEA)

Ulleungdo (S. Korea)
Liancourt Rocks (Dokdo, Takeshima)
Yeongdeok
SOUTH KOREA
Pohang
ULSAN
Korea Strait
Tsushima (Japan)
Oki-Shotō (Japan)

Wakkanai
Rebun-Tō
Rishiri-Tō
Teshio
Embetsu
Haboro
Esashi
Otoineppu
Ōmu
Mombetsu
Yūbetsu
Abashiri-Wan
Abashiri
Rausu Dake 1661
Nayoro
Shibetsu
Engaru
Kitami
Shari
Nakashibetsu
Rumoi
Asahikawa
Daisetsu-Zan 2290
2077
Takikawa
Akabira
Bibai
Iwamizawa
Hokkaidō
Shibecha
Honbetsu
Kushiro
Ishikari-Wan
Atsuta
Kamui-Misaki
Otaru
SAPPORO
Ebetsu
Obihiro
Poroshiri-Dake 2052
Iwanai
Shikotsu-Ko
Chitose
Toya-Ko
Suttsu
Tomakomai
Hiroo
Setana
Uchiura-Wan
Muroran
Urakawa
Samani
Erimo-misaki
Okushiri-Tō
Yakumo
Esan-Misaki
Esashi
Hakodate
Tsugaru Kaikyō
Shiriya-Zaki
Matsumae
Shirakami-Misaki
Ohata
Mutsu
Mutsu-Wan
Kanagi
Aomori
Goshogawara
Towada
Hachinohe
Henashi-Misaki
Hirosaki
Towada-Ko
Ōdate
Kuji
Noshiro
Kazuno
Iwaizumi
Oga-Hantō
Oga
Iwate-San 2041
Morioka
Miyako
Hayachine-San 1914
Akita
Ōmagari
Hanamaki
Kamaishi
Honjō
Chōkai-San 2230
Mizusawa
Kesennuma
Sakata
Ichinoseki
Tsuruoka
Furukawa
Ishinomaki
Gas-San 1980
SENDAI
Sendai-Wan
Sado
Ryōtsu
Murakami
Yamagata
Aikawa
Niigata
Nagai
Shibata
Sōma
Fukushima
Haranomachi
Niitsu
Higashiazuma-San 2024
Sanjo
Aizuwakamatsu
Koriyama
Honshū
Nagaoka
Sukagawa
Iwaki
Suzu-Misaki
Wajima
Suzu
Toyama-Wan
Tōkamachi
Tajima
Tanakura
Kitaibaraki
Nanao
Takada
Shirane-San 2578
Yaita
Hitachi
Hakui
Himi
Iiyama
Nagano
Kiryū
Utsunomiya
Mito
Toyama
Kusatsu
8412
Takaoka
Hodaka-Dake 3190
Maebashi
Oyama
Kanazawa
Takasaki
Tsuchiura
Matsumoto
Kumagaya
SAITAMA
Komatsu
Takayama
Kawagoe
Kawaguchi
Fukui
Haku-San 2702
Ontake-San 3063
Kofu
TOKYO
Funabashi
Chiba
Echizen-Misaki
Takefu
Gero
KAWASAKI
YOKOHAMA
Ichihara
Kyō-ga-Saki
Wakasa-Wan
Tsuruga
Gifu
Iida
Fuji-San 3776
Odawara
Yokosuka
Tottori
Toyooka
Obama
Ogaki
Ichinomiya
Fuji
Numazu
Tateyama
Nojima-Zaki
Matsue
Yonago
Dai-Sen 1729
Maizuru
Biwa-Ko
NAGOYA
Toyota
Shizuoka
Itō
Izumo
Fukuchiyama
Ayabe
KYOTO
Otsu
Okazaki
Toyohashi
Suruga-Wan
Ō-Shima
Ōda
Tsuyama
Yokkaichi
Iwata
Irō-Zaki
Nii-Jima
Izu-Shotō
Chūgoku-Sanchi
Himeji
Nishinomiya
Higashiōsaka
Hamamatsu
Omae-Zaki
Hamada
Miyoshi
Okayama
KOBE
Amagasaki
OSAKA
Matsusaka
Ise-Wan
Miyake-Jima
9076
Masuda
Fuchū
Izumi-Sano
Daiō-Misaki
HIROSHIMA
Fukuyama
Takamatsu
Awaji-Shima
Naruto
Wakayama
Hagi
Iwakuni
Kure
Marugame
Tokushima
1915
Owase
Yamaguchi
Imabari
Ikeda
Anan
Kii-Sanchi
Ube
Tokuyama
1955
Kii-Suidō
Gobō
Shingū
Hōfu
Matsuyama
Tsurugi-San
Mugi
Tanabe
Kushimoto
Shimonoseki
Shikoku-Sanchi
Nankoku
Hachijō-Jima
Katsumoto
KITAKYŪSHŪ
Kōchi
Muroto
Shio-no-Misaki
Iki
Nōgata
Bungotakada
Tosa-Wan
Muroto-Misaki
FUKUOKA
Buzen
Beppu
Yawatahama
Karatsu
Saga
Ōita
Uwajima
Shikoku
Imari
Kurume
Kuju-San 1787
Nakamura
PACIFIC OCEAN
Nampō-shotō
Aoga-Shima
Gotō-Rettō
Sasebo
Ōmuta
Bungo-Suidō
Kumamoto
Saiki
Sukumo
Isahaya
Ashizuri-Zaki
Nagasaki
Nobeoka
Yatsushiro
Kyūshū-Sanchi
Fukue-Shima
Hondo
Hyūga
Amakusa-Shotō
Ushibuka
Kyūshū
Minamata
Miyazaki
Kurino
Koshiki-Rettō
Sendai
Miyakonojō
Nichinan
Kagoshima
Kanoya
Makurazaki
Ibusuki
Sata-Misaki

m ft
0
200 600
2000 6000
4000 12 000
6000 18 000
8000 24 000

Projection: Conical with two standard parallels
East from Greenwich

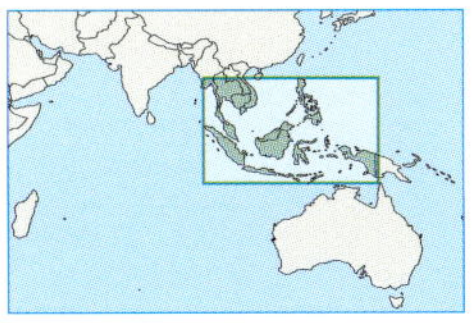

1:20 000 000

100 0 100 200 300 400 500 600 700 800 km

100 0 100 200 300 400 500 miles

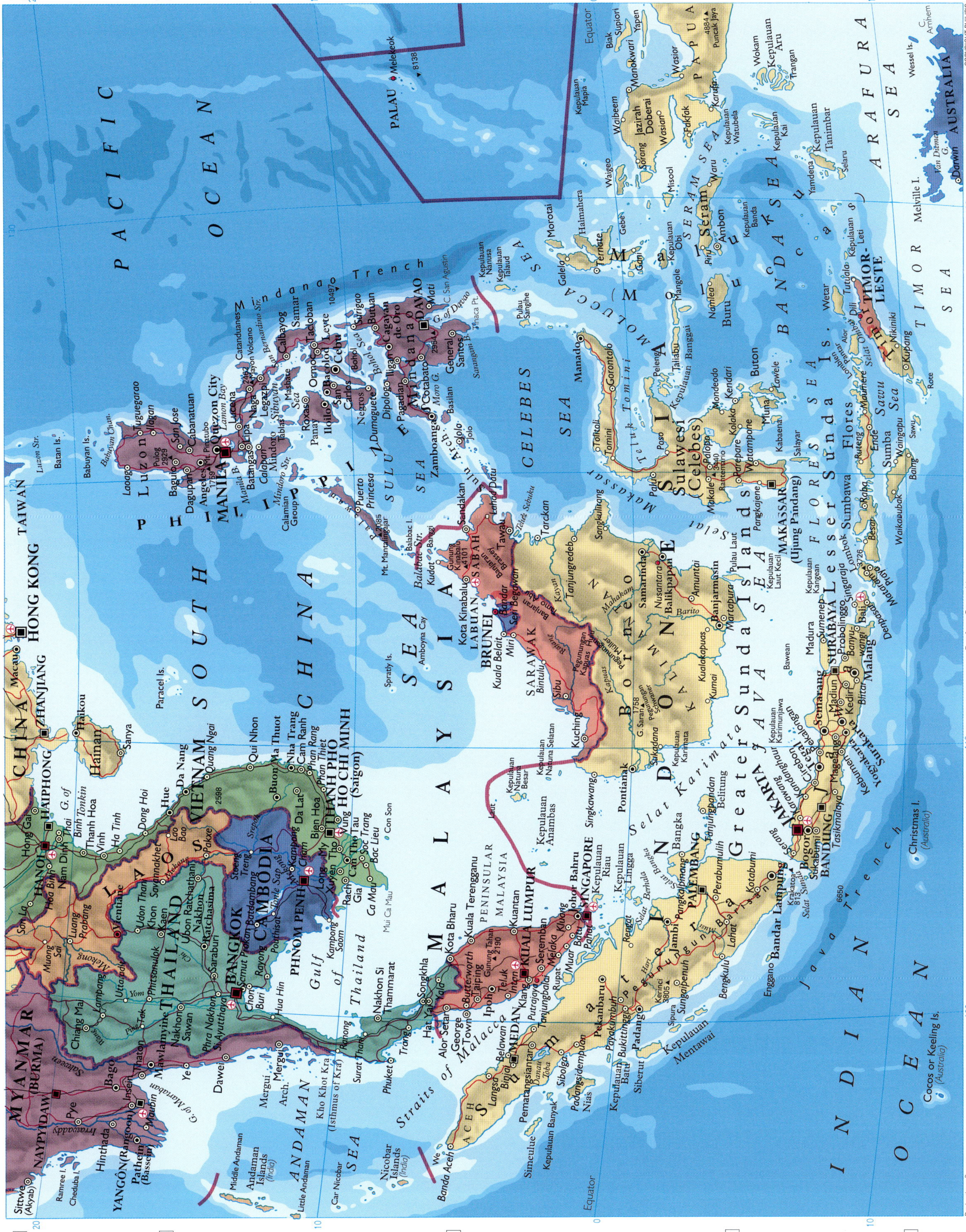

Projection: Bonne

East from Greenwich

0 200 600 2000 6000 4000 12 000 6000 18 000 8000 24 000

m ft

30

1:17 500 000
Projection: Bonne
East from Greenwich
TURKEY
SYRIA
IRAQ
IRAN
SAUDI ARABIA
YEMEN
OMAN
ETHIOPIA
SOMALIA
AFGHANISTAN
TURKMENISTAN
UZBEKISTAN
KENYA
ERITREA
JORDAN
LEBANON
ISRAEL
EGYPT
SUDAN
KUWAIT
QATAR
UNITED ARAB EMIRATES
DJIBOUTI
CYPRUS
Mediterranean Sea
Black Sea
Caspian Sea
Red Sea
Persian Gulf
Gulf of Oman
Gulf of Aden
ARABIAN SEA
INDIAN
Rub' al Khālī (Empty Quarter)
An Nafūd (Nafud Desert)
ANKARA
TEHRĀN
BAGHDĀD
AR RIYĀD (Riyadh)
SAN'Ā'
ADDIS ABABA (Addis Abeba)
MUQDISHO (Mogadishu)
KARACHI
Masqat (Muscat)
DUBAYY (Dubai)
AL KUWAYT (Kuwait)
Socotra (Yemen)

KYRGYZSTAN
Bishkek
Taraz
Osh
Andijon
Farghona
Kashi
XINJIANG UYGUR ZIZHIQU
(SINKIANG)
Taklamakan Shamo
Tarim Pendi (Tarim Basin)
Lop Nur
Korla
Kuruktag
Aksu
Yarkant
Hotan
Yutian
Qiemo
Ruoqiang
Altun Shan
Kunlun Shan
Aksai Chin
Karakoram Ra.
Gilgit
Chitral
Nanga Parbat
K2
Qilian Shan
Qaidam Pendi
Hoh Xil Shan
Golmud
QINGHAI
Xining
Lanzhou
Tianshui
Baoji
Xi'an
Bayan Har Shan
Qinghai Hu (Koko Nor)
Yumen
Zhangye
Jiuquan
Dunhuang
NEI MONGOL ZIZHIQU (INNER MONGOLIA)
Yinchuan
Wuzhong
Shizuishan
NINGXIA HUIZU ZIZHIQU
Yan'an
Tongchuan
Xianyang
Hanzhong
Guangyuan
Dazhou
Nanchong
Mianyang
CHENGDU
CHONGQING
SICHUAN
Leshan
Zigong
Neijiang
Suining
Yibin
Xichang
Zhaotong
GUIZHOU
Liupanshui
Anshun
Qujing
KUNMING
YUNNAN
Dali
Baoshan
Tengchong
Panzhihua
Gejiu
Kaiyuan
Jinghong
Simao
CHINA
XIZANG ZIZHIQU
(TIBET)
Tanggula Shan
(Dangla Range)
Nyainqentanglha Shan
Lhasa
Xigazê
Qamdo
Nam Co
Siling Co
Mapam Yumco
Yarlung Zangbo Jiang
Namcha Barwa 7756
Himalaya
Mt. Everest 8849
Annapurna
Dhaulagiri
NEPAL
KATHMANDU
Pokhara
Biratnagar
BHUTAN
Thimphu
SIKKIM
Darjiling
ARUNACHAL PRADESH
ASSAM
NAGALAND
MANIPUR
MIZORAM
MEGHALAYA
TRIPURA
Guwahati
Dibrugarh
Imphal
Silchar
BANGLADESH
DHAKA (Dacca)
Rajshahi
Khulna
Barisal
Chattogram
Sylhet
Rangpur
SRINAGAR
JAMMU & KASHMIR
LADAKH
Leh
Jammu
Islamabad
Rawalpindi
Sialkot
Gujranwala
LAHORE
Multan
Amritsar
Jullundur
Ludhiana
Chandigarh
HIMACHAL PRADESH
PUNJAB
HARYANA
UTTARAKHAND
Dehra Dun
Haridwar
Saharanpur
Meerut
DELHI
New Delhi
Ghaziabad
Faridabad
Moradabad
Bareilly
Shahjahanpur
Aligarh
Mathura
Agra
UTTAR PRADESH
LUCKNOW
KANPUR
PRAYAGRAJ
VARANASI
Gorakhpur
Patna
BIHAR
Bhagalpur
Gaya
JHARKHAND
DHANBAD
Ranchi
ASANSOL
JAMSHEDPUR
KOLKATA (Calcutta)
Haora
Kharagpur
Sundarbans
RAJASTHAN
Jodhpur
Ajmer
Jaipur
Bikaner
Kota
Udaipur
Gwalior
Jhansi
MADHYA PRADESH
Bhopal
Indore
Ujjain
Jabalpur
Sagar
AHMADABAD
Vadodara
Surat
Rajkot
GUJARAT
Vindhya Range
Satpura Range
Narmada
NAGPUR
Raipur
Bhilainagar
Durg
Bilaspur
Raurkela
CHHATTISGARH
ODISHA
Cuttack
Bhubaneshwar
Puri
Brahmapur (Berhampur)
VISHAKHAPATNAM
Rajahmahendravaram
Kakinada
MAHARASHTRA
MUMBAI (Bombay)
Thane
Nashik
Aurangabad
Jalna
Akola
Amravati
PUNE (Poona)
SOLAPUR
Ahmadnagar
Kolhapur
Sangli
TELANGANA
HYDERABAD
Warangal
Nizamabad
VIJAYAWADA
Guntur
Eluru
Kurnool
ANDHRA PRADESH
Nellore
Anantapur
GOA
Panaji
Belagavi
Dharwad
Hubballi
Ballari
Davangere
Shivamogga
Udupi
KARNATAKA
Mangaluru
Mysuru
BENGALURU (Bangalore)
Kolar
CHENNAI (Madras)
Puducherry (Pondicherry)
Salem
TAMIL NADU
Coimbatore
Tiruchchirappalli
Kumbakonam
Madurai
Tuticorin
Tirunelveli
Kozhikode (Calicut)
Palghat
KOCHI (Cochin)
Alappuzha
Kollam
Thiruvananthapuram
Nagercoil
KERALA
Kanyakumari (C. Comorin)
Western Ghats
Eastern Ghats
Malabar Coast
Coromandel Coast
Palk Strait
G. of Mannar
Jaffna
Trincomalee
Batticaloa
Kandy
SRI LANKA
Colombo
Sri Jayewardenepura Kotte
Dehiwala
Moratuwa
Galle
Dondra Head
MALDIVES
Malé
Minicoy I. (India)
Bay of Bengal
Andaman Is. (India)
North Andaman
Middle Andaman
South Andaman
Port Blair
Little Andaman
Ten Degree Channel
Car Nicobar
Nicobar Is. (India)
Great Nicobar
Great Channel
Preparis Is.
Coco Is.
Andaman Sea
Myeik Kyunzu (Mergui Arch.)
MYANMAR (BURMA)
Kachin
Myitkyina
Lashio
Mandalay
Monywa
Myingyan
Meiktila
Taunggyi
Shan
Sittwe (Akyab)
Ramree I.
Cheduba I.
Arakan Yoma
Pegu Yoma
NAY PYI TAW
Pyinmana
Toungoo
Pyay
Hinthada
Pathein (Bassein)
YANGON (Rangoon)
Bago
Mawlamyine
G. of Martaban
Dawei
Mergui
Ranong
LAOS
Luang Prabang
Vientiane (Viangchan)
Chiang Mai
Lampang
Udon Thani
Khon Kaen
THAILAND
Nakhon Ratchasima
BANGKOK
Rayong
Gulf of Thailand
Chumphon
Kho Khot Kra (Isthmus of Kra)
Surat Thani
Nakhon Si Thammarat
Phuket
Hat Yai
Songkla
Malay Pen.
Kota Bharu
Kuala Terengganu
Kuantan
George Town
Ipoh
MALAYSIA
KUALA LUMPUR
Putrajaya
Johor Bharu
SINGAPORE
Straits of Malacca
Banda Aceh
Aceh
MEDAN
Tanjungbalai
Pematangsiantar
Simeulue
INDONESIA
VIETNAM
CAMBODIA
INDIAN OCEAN
m ft
200 600
1000 3000
2000 6000
3000 9000
4000 12 000

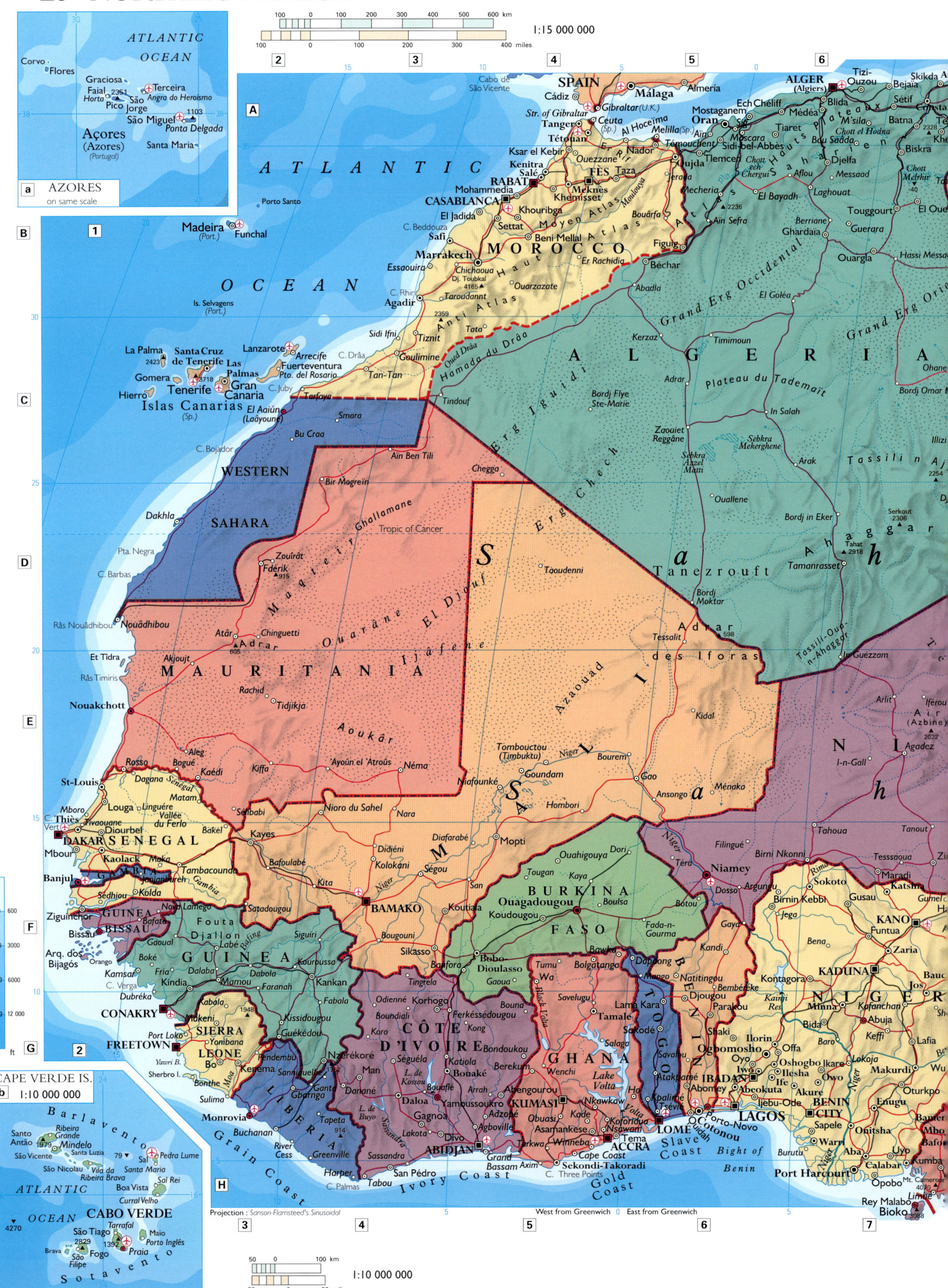
1:15 000 000
km
miles
ATLANTIC
OCEAN
Corvo
Flores
Graciosa
Terceira
Faial
Horta
São Jorge
Angra do Heroísmo
Pico
São Miguel
Ponta Delgada
Açores
(Azores)
(Portugal)
Santa Maria
a AZORES
on same scale
SPAIN
Cádiz
Málaga
Almería
Gibraltar (U.K.)
Str. of Gibraltar
Tanger
Ceuta
Tétouan
Al Hoceima
Melilla (Sp.)
Nador
Cabo de São Vicente
ALGER
(Algiers)
Tizi-Ouzou
Bejaïa
Skikda
Blida
Ech Chéliff
Médéa
Sétif
Mostaganem
Oran
Tiaret
Batna
M'sila
Chott el Hodna
Biskra
Tlemcen
Sidi-bel-Abbès
Mascara
Djelfa
Oujda
Témouchent
Taza
FÈS
Meknès
Khemisset
Ouezzane
Kenitra
Salé
RABAT
Ksar el Kebir
Mohammedia
CASABLANCA
El Jadida
Khouribga
Settat
Safi
Beni-Mellal
Marrakech
Essaouira
MOROCCO
Er Rachidia
Figuig
Béchar
Chichaoua
Dj. Toubkal
4165
Ouarzazate
Taroudannt
Agadir
Tiznit
Sidi Ifni
Tata
Goulimine
Tan-Tan
Tarfaya
C. Drâa
C. Juby
Hamada du Drâa
Madeira
(Port.)
Funchal
Porto Santo
Is. Selvagens
(Port.)
OCEAN
ATLANTIC
La Palma
Santa Cruz de Tenerife
Lanzarote
Arrecife
Fuerteventura
Pto. del Rosario
Las Palmas
Gran Canaria
Gomera
Tenerife
Hierro
Islas Canarias
(Sp.)
El Aaiún
(Laâyoune)
Smara
Bu Craa
C. Bojador
WESTERN
SAHARA
Dakhla
Pta. Negra
C. Barbas
Aïn Ben Tili
Bir Mogreïn
Chegga
Tindouf
Zouîrât
Fdérik
915
Tropic of Cancer
Nouâdhibou
Râs Nouâdhibou
Atâr
Chinguetti
Adrar
Akjoujt
Et Tidra
Râs Timiris
MAURITANIA
Nouakchott
Rachid
Tidjikja
Aoukâr
Aleg
Boguè
Kaédi
Kiffa
'Ayoûn el 'Atroûs
Néma
Rosso
St-Louis
Dagana
Matam
Louga
Linguère
Sélibabi
SENEGAL
Thiès
Diourbel
DAKAR
Mbour
Kaolack
Tambacounda
Bakel
Kayes
Banjul
GAMBIA
Kolda
Ziguinchor
GUINEA-BISSAU
Bissau
Bafatá
Arq. dos Bijagós
Fouta Djallon
GUINEA
Boké
Labé
Kindia
Mamou
Dabola
Faranah
Kankan
Siguiri
Kouroussa
CONAKRY
Kissidougou
Guékédou
Kabala
SIERRA LEONE
Makeni
FREETOWN
Port Loko
Yonibana
Bo
Kenema
Sherbro I.
Bonthe
Sulima
Monrovia
Buchanan
LIBERIA
Gbarnga
Nzérékoré
Harper
Greenville
River Cess
Grain Coast
C. Palmas
MALI
Tombouctou
(Timbuktu)
Goundam
Niafounké
Bourem
Gao
Kidal
Tessalit
Adrar des Iforas
Azaouad
Ansongo
Ménaka
Hombori
Mopti
Nioro du Sahel
Nara
Diafarabé
Ségou
San
Koutiala
BAMAKO
Kita
Bafoulabé
Bougouni
Sikasso
Taoudenni
Erg Chech
El Djouf
Ouarâne
Maqteïr
Ijâfene
Tanezrouft
Bordj Moktar
ALGERIA
Abadla
Kerzaz
Timimoun
Adrar
Reggane
Zaouiet Reggâne
In Salah
Plateau du Tademaït
Grand Erg Occidental
Grand Erg Oriental
El Goléa
Ghardaïa
Ouargla
Touggourt
Laghouat
El Bayadh
Aïn Sefra
Arak
Tassili n Ajjer
Tamanrasset
Ahaggar
Serkout
Tahat
2918
Bordj in Eker
Ouallene
Tassili-Oua-n-Ahaggar
In Guezzam
Erg Iguidi
Bordj Flye Ste-Marie
NIGER
Arlit
Iférouane
Aïr
(Azbine)
Agadez
I-n-Gall
Tahoua
Tanout
Filingué
Niamey
Tillabéry
Dosso
Birni Nkonni
Maradi
Zinder
BURKINA FASO
Ouagadougou
Ouahigouya
Kaya
Dori
Koudougou
Boulsa
Fada-n-Gourma
Bobo-Dioulasso
Banfora
Gaoua
CÔTE D'IVOIRE
Korhogo
Odienné
Boundiali
Ferkéssédougou
Séguéla
Katiola
Bouaké
Bondoukou
Man
Danané
Daloa
Yamoussoukro
Gagnoa
Divo
Agboville
ABIDJAN
Sassandra
San Pédro
Tabou
Grand Bassam
Ivory Coast
GHANA
Bolgatanga
Tamale
Lake Volta
Kumasi
Obuasi
Koforidua
ACCRA
Tema
Cape Coast
Sekondi-Takoradi
Axim
C. Three Points
Gold Coast
TOGO
Dapaong
Kara
Sokodé
Atakpamé
Kpalimé
LOMÉ
BENIN
Natitingou
Djougou
Parakou
Kandi
Porto-Novo
Cotonou
Abomey
Slave Coast
Bight of Benin
NIGERIA
Sokoto
Gusau
Birnin Kebbi
KANO
Katsina
Zaria
KADUNA
Minna
Abuja
Ilorin
Ogbomosho
Oyo
Iwo
IBADAN
Abeokuta
Ijebu-Ode
LAGOS
Osogbo
Akure
BENIN CITY
Onitsha
Enugu
Makurdi
Lafia
Port Harcourt
Warri
Aba
Calabar
Uyo
Opobo
Jos
Kafanchan
Bida
Bioko
Rey Malabo
Mt. Cameroon
4070
CAPE VERDE IS.
b 1:10 000 000
Barlavento
Santo Antão
Mindelo
São Vicente
Santa Luzia
São Nicolau
Sal
Pedra Lume
Santa Maria
Boa Vista
Sal Rei
Ribeira Brava
Curral Velho
ATLANTIC
OCEAN
CABO VERDE
São Tiago
Tarrafal
Maio
Porto Inglês
Praia
Fogo
Brava
São Filipe
Sotavento
4270
Projection : Sanson-Flamsteed's Sinusoidal
West from Greenwich
East from Greenwich
1:10 000 000

8 9 10 11 12 13 14
A B C D E F G H
24
28
28

100 0 100 200 300 400 500 600 km

100 0 100 200 300 400 miles

1:15 000 000

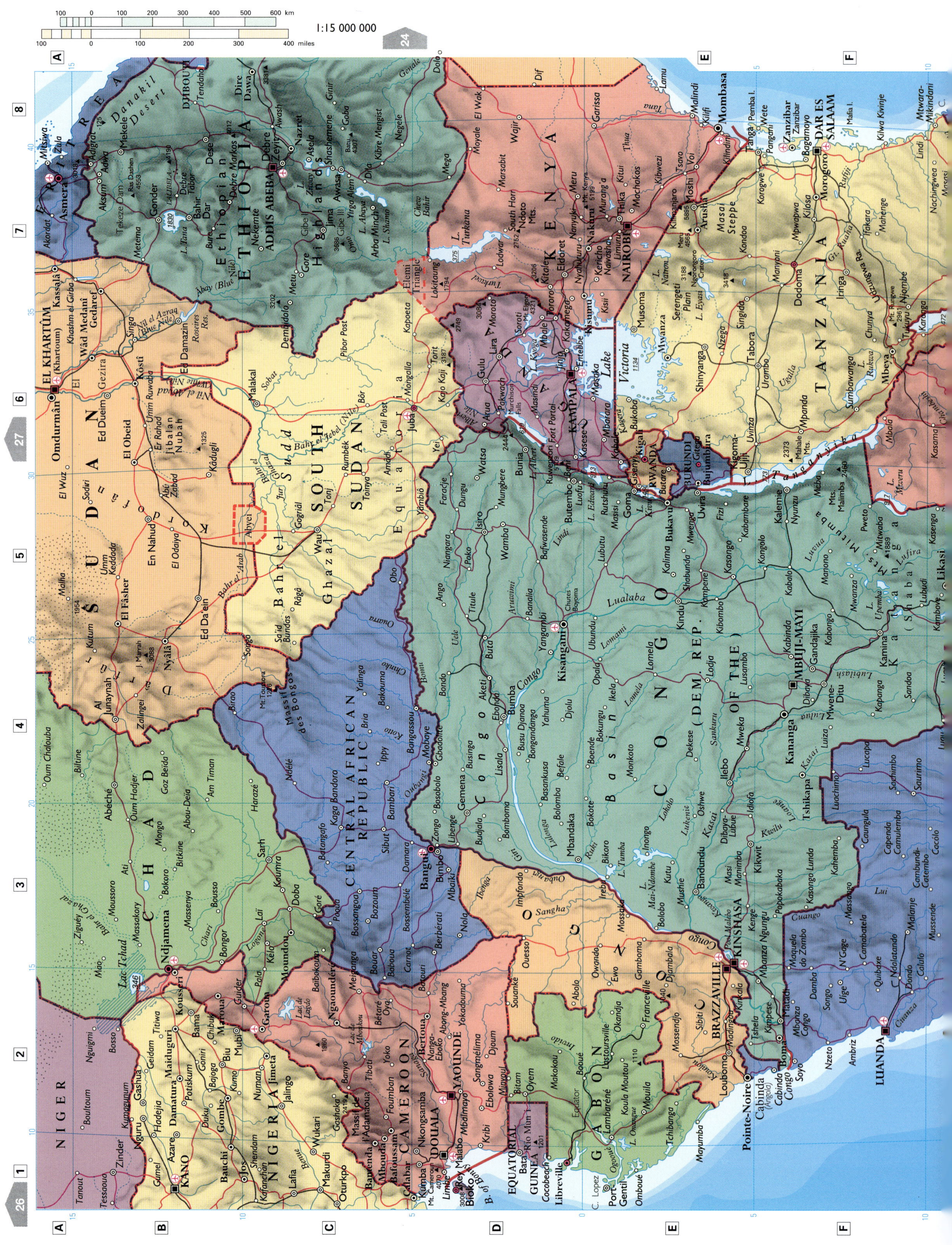

ATLANTIC OCEAN
INDIAN OCEAN
ZAMBIA
ZIMBABWE
MOZAMBIQUE
BOTSWANA
NAMIBIA
SOUTH AFRICA
LESOTHO
ESWATINI
MADAGASCAR
LUSAKA
HARARE
MAPUTO
PRETORIA (Tshwane)
JOHANNESBURG
CAPE TOWN
DURBAN
GQEBERHA (Port Elizabeth)
ANTANANARIVO
Windhoek
Gaborone
Maseru
Lilongwe
Bulawayo
Blantyre
Beira
Kalahari
Namib Desert
Skeleton Coast
Caprivi Strip
Tropic of Capricorn
Mozambique Channel
COMOROS 1:8 000 000 a
SEYCHELLES 1:2 500 000 b
RÉUNION 1:2 500 000 c
MAURITIUS 1:2 500 000 d
MADAGASCAR on same scale as main map
1:2 500 000
1:8 000 000
Projection Sanson-Flamsteed's Sinusoidal
COPYRIGHT PHILIPS

1:20 000 000
Projection: Lambert's Equivalent Azimuthal
East from Greenwich
INDONESIA
PAPUA NEW GUINEA
AUSTRALIA
WESTERN AUSTRALIA
NORTHERN TERRITORY
QUEENSLAND
SOUTH AUSTRALIA
NEW SOUTH WALES
VICTORIA
TASMANIA
A.C.T.
TIMOR-LESTE
New Guinea
Papua
Arafura Sea
Timor Sea
Banda Sea
Flores Sea
Savu Sea
Seram Sea
Bismarck Sea
Coral Sea
Gulf of Carpentaria
Gulf of Papua
Torres Strait
Great Australian Bight
Bass Strait
INDIAN OCEAN
SOUTHERN OCEAN
South Australian Basin
North Australia Basin
Naturaliste Plateau
Queensland Plateau
Great Barrier Reef
Great Dividing Range
Great Sandy Desert
Gibson Desert
Great Victoria Desert
Tanami Desert
Simpson Desert
Sturt Stony Desert
Nullarbor Plain
Barkly Tableland
MacDonnell Ranges
Musgrave Ranges
Hamersley Range
Darling Range
Flinders Ranges
Snowy Mts.
Kimberley
Arnhem Land
Cape York Peninsula
PERTH
ADELAIDE
MELBOURNE
Canberra
SYDNEY
BRISBANE
Darwin
Hobart
Cairns
Townsville
Alice Springs
Port Moresby
MAKASSAR (UJUNG PANDANG)
Mt. Kosciuszko 2228
Mt. Zeil 1531
Uluru (Ayers Rock) 867
Puncak Jaya 4884
Mt. Wilhelm 4508
Mt. Ossa 1617
Lake Eyre
Lake Torrens
Lake Gairdner
Murray
Darling
Kangaroo I.
Melville I.
Groote Eylandt
Flinders I.
King I.
C. York
C. Leeuwin
C. Howe
S.E.Cape
South Tasman Plateau
Tasman Abyssal

10 11 12 13 14 15 16

Ontong Java Plateau
Solomon Rise
Melanesia
Bougainville
Choiseul
SOLOMON ISLANDS
Santa Isabel
New Georgia Is.
Vangunu
Russell Is.
Florida Is.
Malaita
Honiara
2439
Guadalcanal
San Cristóbal (Makira)
Pocklington Reef
Bellona
Rennell
South Solomon Trench
7223
Reef Is.
Duff Is.
Nendo
Santa Cruz Is.
Vanikoro
9165
Vitiaz Trench
Fataka
Tikopia
Is. Torres
Vanua Lava
Is. Banks
Gaua
Espíritu Santo
1879
Malakula
VANUATU (New Hebrides)
Epi
Shepherd Is.
Port Vila
Efate
Erromango
Tanna
Aneityum
Îles D'Entrecasteaux
Îles Bélep
Îles Chesterfield
New Caledonia (Fr.)
1628
Î. Lifou
Î. Maré
Îles Loyauté
Nouméa
Î. des Pins
South New Hebrides Trench
7569
Î. Matthew
West Fiji Basin
Rotuma
Vanua Levu
Viti Levu
1323
Suva
FIJI
Kadavu
Taveuni
Lau Group
Lau Ridge
Lau Basin
Ceva-i-Ra
Tabiteuea
Beru
Nikunau
Gilbert Is.
Tamana
Arorae
KIRIBATI
6195
Namumea
Nanumanga
Niutao
Nui
Vaitupu
TUVALU (Ellice Is.)
Funafuti
Fongafale
Nukulaelae
Niulakita
Baker (U.S.A.)
Equator
McKean
Abariringa
Birnie
Enderbury
Nikumaroro
Phoenix Is.
Orona
Rawaki
Carondelet
Manra
Atafu
Nukunonu
Tokelau Is. (N.Z.)
Fakaofo
International Date Line
Mata-Utu
Uvea
Wallis & Futuna (Fr.)
Horn
Alofi
SAMOA
Savai'i
'Upolu
Apia
Pago Pago
Tutuila
American Samoa (U.S.A.)
Niuafo'ou
Niua Group
Niuatoputapu
Vava'u Group
Late
Ha'apai Group
TONGA
Nuku'alofa
Tongatapu Group
Eua
Ata
Niue (N.Z.)
Tonga Trench
10 882
Tropic of Capricorn
PACIFIC OCEAN
5303
South Fiji Basin
Lord Howe Seamount Chain
Caledonia
Norfolk Ridge
Norfolk I. (Austral.)
Norfolk Basin
Lord Howe I. (Austral.)
734
Lord Howe Rise
Trough
Tasman Sea
Raoul I.
Kermadec Is. (N.Z.)
Macauley I.
Curtis I.
Colville Ridge
10 047
Kermadec Trench
International Date Line
Southwest Pacific Basin
North C.
Kaitaia
Whangarei
AUCKLAND
North Island
Challenger Plateau
Hamilton
Bay of Plenty
Tauranga
New Plymouth
Rotorua
Gisborne
Ruapehu
2797
Napier
NEW ZEALAND
Wanganui
Palmerston North
Masterton
Nelson
Cook Strait
Blenheim
Wellington
5267
Greymouth
South Island
Aoraki/Mt. Cook
3724
Southern Alps
Christchurch
Chatham Rise
Chatham I.
Chatham Is. (N.Z.)
Pitt I.
Queenstown
Timaru
Dunedin
Invercargill
Stewart I.

A B C D E F G H J

160 165 170 175 West from Greenwich 170 165 160

0 5 10 15 20 25 30 35 40 45

10 11 12 13 14 15 16 17 18

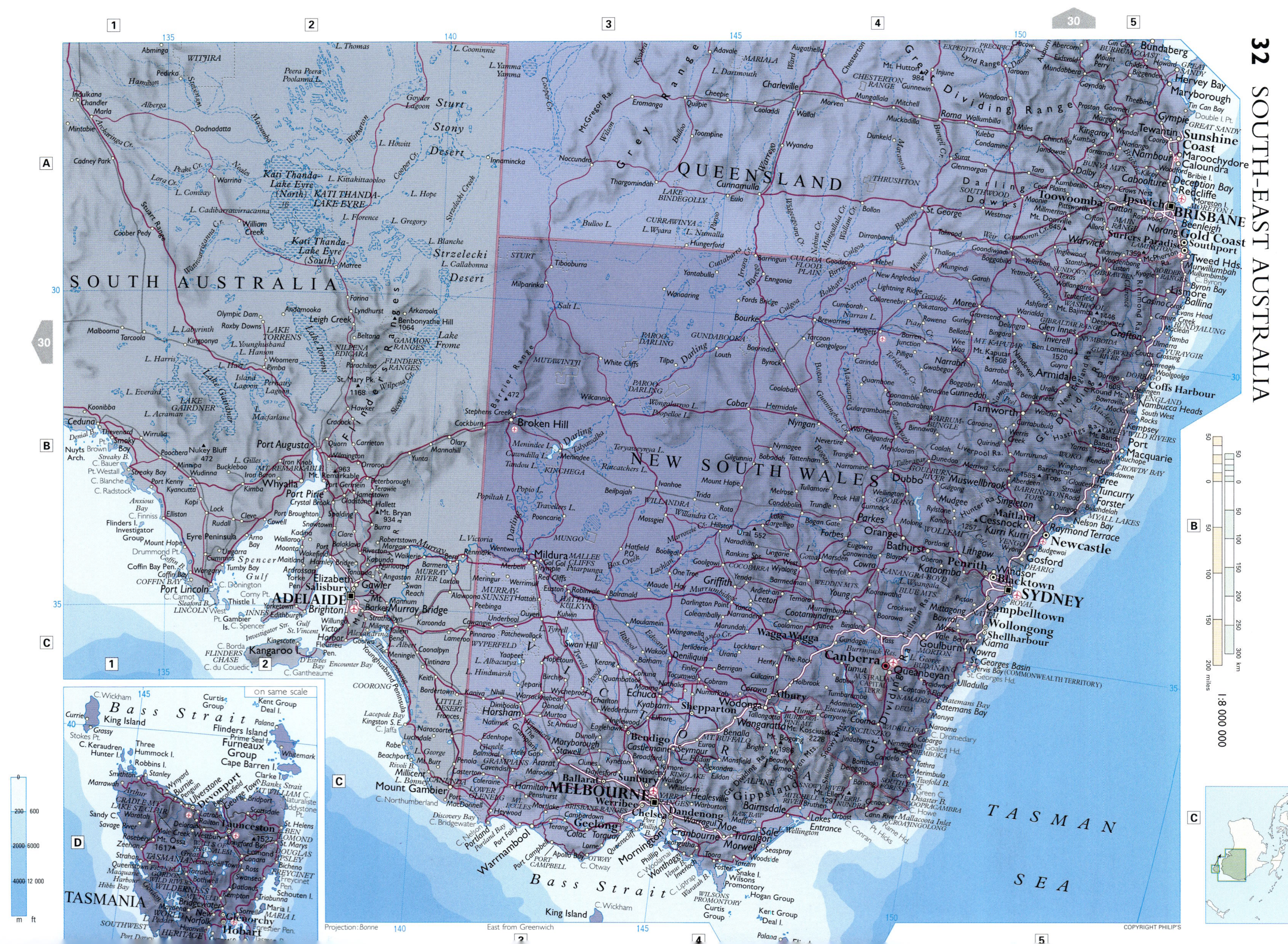

1:8 000 000
QUEENSLAND
NEW SOUTH WALES
SOUTH AUSTRALIA
TASMANIA
TASMAN SEA
Bass Strait
SYDNEY
MELBOURNE
ADELAIDE
BRISBANE
Canberra
Hobart
Newcastle
Wollongong
Broken Hill
Port Augusta
Mount Gambier
King Island
Flinders Island
Kangaroo I.
on same scale
Projection: Bonne
East from Greenwich
COPYRIGHT PHILIP'S
m ft

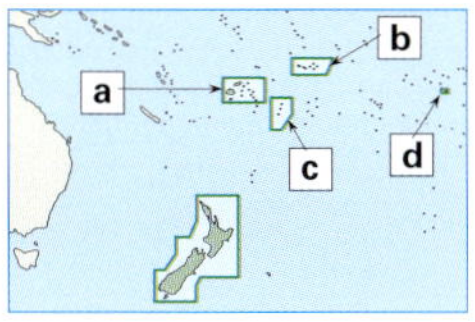

1:6 000 000

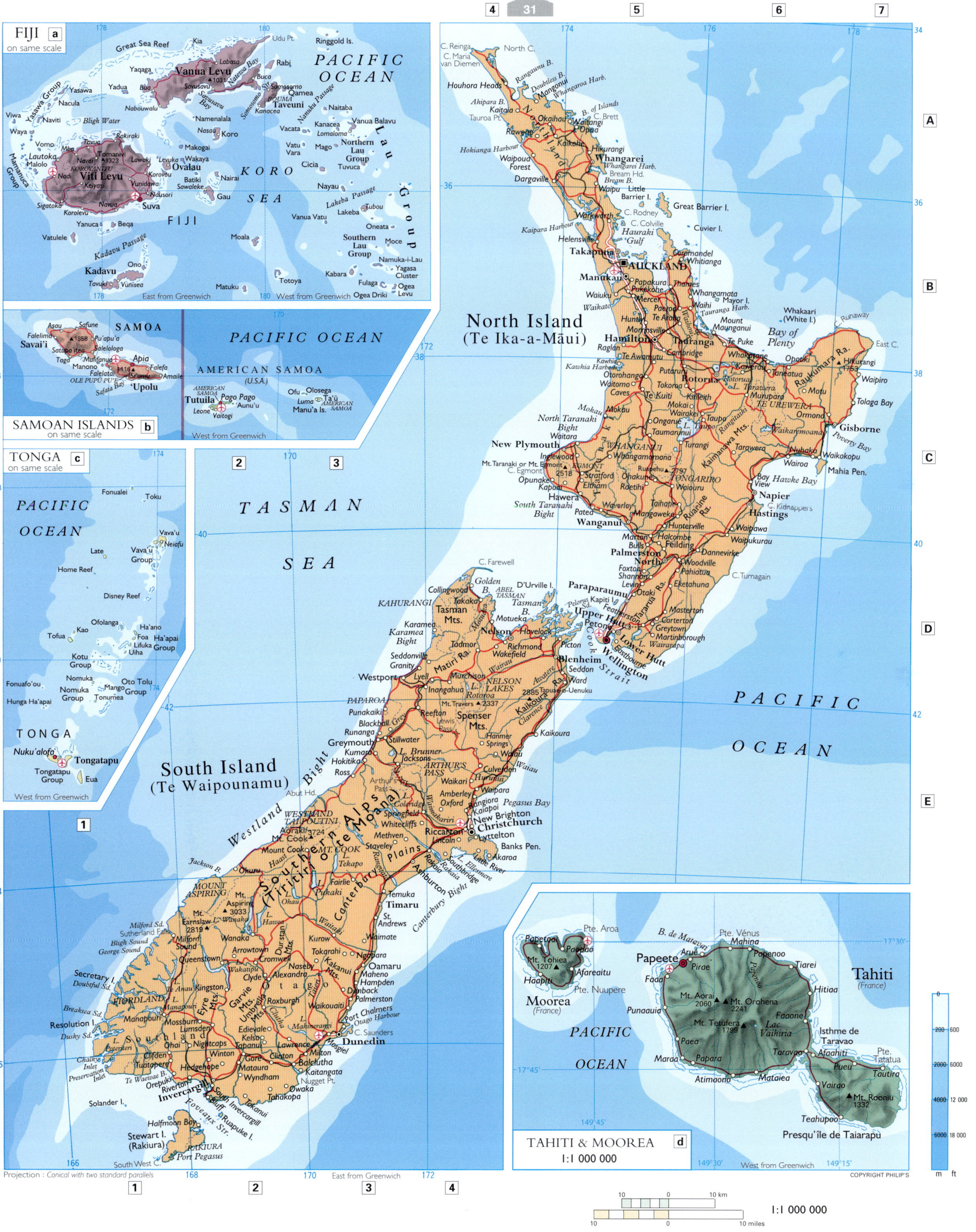

50 0 50 100 150 200 km

50 0 50 100 150 miles

4 31 5 6 7

FIJI a
on same scale

Great Sea Reef
Kia
Udu Pt.
Ringgold Is.
Labasa
Vanua Levu
Natewa Bay
Rabi
PACIFIC OCEAN
Yaqaga
Bua
Savusavu
Buca
Yasawa Group
Yasawa
Yadua
Somosomo Str.
Qamea
Taveuni
Nabouwalu
Savusavu Bay
BOUMA
Kanacea
Nanuku Passage
Naitaba
Nacula
Viwa
Naviti
Bligh Water
Namenalala
Vanua Balavu
Waya
Rakiraki
Nasau
Koro
Vacata
Kanacea
Lomaloma
Vomo
Tavua
Makogai
Vatu Vara
Mago
Northern Lau Group
Lautoka
Malolo
Navai
Tomanivi 1323
Lawaki
Levuka
Wakaya
Ovalau
Cicia
Tuvuca
KORO SEA
Mamanuca Group
KOROYANITU
Viti Levu
Korovou
Batiki
Nairai
Nadi
Keiyasi
Vunidawa
Sawaleke
Nayau
Nausori
Gau
Lakeba Passage
Sigatoka
Navua
Suva
Tubou
Korolevu
Vanua Vatu
Lakeba
Lau Group
Yanuca
Beqa
FIJI
Oneata
Vatulele
Moala
Southern Lau Group
Moce
Kadavu Passage
Namuka-i-Lau
Ono
Yagasa Cluster
Kadavu
Totoya
Kabara
Fulaga
Ogea
Tavuki
Vunisea
Matuku
Ogea Driki
Levu
178
180
East from Greenwich
West from Greenwich

SAMOAN ISLANDS b
on same scale

Asau
Safune
SAMOA
Falelima
Savai'i
1858
Pu'apu'a
Salelologa
Satupa'itea
Apia
Mulifanua
Falefa
Tago
Manono
1116
Faleatai
Siumu
Amaile
OLE PUPU PU'E
Safata Bay
Upolu
PACIFIC OCEAN
AMERICAN SAMOA (U.S.A.)
AMERICAN SAMOA
Tutuila
Pago Pago
'Aunu'u
Leone
Vaitogi
Ofu
Olosega
Ta'u
Luma
AMERICAN SAMOA
Manu'a Is.
170
172
West from Greenwich

TONGA c
on same scale

PACIFIC OCEAN
Fonualei
Toku
Vava'u
Neiafu
Late
Vava'u Group
Home Reef
Disney Reef
Ofolanga
Ha'ano
Kao
Tofua
Foa
Lifuka
Ha'apai Group
Uiha
Kotu Group
Nomuka
Fonuafo'ou
Mango
Oto Tolu Group
Nomuka Group
Tonumea
Hunga Ha'apai
TONGA
Nuku'alofa
Tongatapu
Tongatapu Group
Eua
174
West from Greenwich

North Island (Te Ika-a-Māui)

C. Reinga
North C.
C. Maria van Diemen
Rangaunu B.
Houhora Heads
Doubtless B.
Mangonui
Whangaroa Harb.
Ahipara B.
Kaitaia
Tauroa Pt.
B. of Islands
Okaihau
C. Brett
Rawene
Waitangi
Opua
Northland
Kaikohe
Hokianga Harbour
Waipoua Forest
Hikurangi
Whangarei
Whangarei Harb.
Bream Hd.
Bream B.
Dargaville
Waipu
Little Barrier I.
Great Barrier I.
C. Rodney
Warkworth
C. Colville
Kaipara Harbour
Hauraki Gulf
Cuvier I.
Helensville
Takapuna
Coromandel
Whitianga
AUCKLAND
Manukau
Papakura
Pukekohe
Thames
Waiuku
Whangamata
Mayor I.
Mercer
Waihi
Tauranga Harb.
Waikato
Paeroa
Te Aroha
Mount Maunganui
Whakaari (White I.)
Runaway
Huntly
Morrinsville
Bay of Plenty
Hamilton
Tauranga
Te Puke
East C.
Raglan
Cambridge
Whakatane
Hikurangi 1753
Te Awamutu
Opotiki
Kawhia
Kawerau
Te Teko
Raukumara Ra.
Waipiro
Kawhia Harbour
Otorohanga
Putaruru
Rotorua
Waitomo Caves
Tokoroa
L. Rotorua
Motu
Tolaga Bay
Te Kuiti
Kinleith
L. Tarawera
Murupara
Mokau
Mokai
TE UREWERA
Ormond
North Taranaki Bight
Waitara
Wairakei
Taupo
L. Taupo
Ongarue
Taumarunui
Rangitaiki Mts.
Waikaremoana
Gisborne
Poverty Bay
New Plymouth
Inglewood
Turangi
Kaimanawa Mts.
Tarawera
WHANGANUI
Nuhaka
Mt. Taranaki or Mt. Egmont 2518
EGMONT
Whangamomona
Ruapehu 2797
Waikokopu
C. Egmont
Stratford
Ohakune
TONGARIRO
Wairoa
Mahia Pen.
Opunake
Eltham
Raetihi
Waiouru
Hawke Bay
Kaponga
Bay View
Hawera
Napier
South Taranaki Bight
Patea
Taihape
Waverley
Mangaweka
Ruahine Ra.
C. Kidnappers
Hastings
Wanganui
Hunterville
Waipawa
Marton
Bulls
Feilding
Waipukurau
Palmerston North
Halcombe
Foxton
Shannon
Dannevirke
Woodville
Pahiatua
C. Turnagain
Levin
Eketahuna
Tararua Ra.
Paraparaumu
Kapiti I.
Otaki
Masterton
Carterton
Greytown
Martinborough
Wairarapa
Upper Hutt
Featherston
Lower Hutt
Porirua
Petone
Wellington
Eastbourne
Cook Strait

TASMAN SEA

PACIFIC OCEAN

South Island (Te Waipounamu)

C. Farewell
Golden B.
D'Urville I.
ABEL TASMAN
Collingwood
Takaka
KAHURANGI
Tasman B.
Pelorus Sd.
Tasman Mts.
Motueka
Karamea
Karamea Bight
Nelson
Havelock
Richmond
Picton
Tadmor
Wakefield
Seddonville
Blenheim
Granity
Matiri Ra.
Wairau
Seddon
Westport
Lyell
Murchison
Awatere
Ward
NELSON LAKES
Inangahua
L. Rotoroa
Tapuae-o-Uenuku 2885
PAPAROA
Mt. Travers 2337
Kaikoura Ra.
Punakaiki
Reefton
Clarence
Blackball
Grey
Lewis Pass
Spenser Mts.
Runanga
Kaikoura
Greymouth
Stillwater
Hanmer Springs
L. Brunner
Kumara
Jacksons
Hokitika
ARTHUR'S PASS
Waiau
Culverden
Ross
Arthur's Pass
Hurunui
Waikari
Amberley
Abut Hd.
Coleridge
Oxford
Rangiora
Waipara
Pegasus Bay
Kaiapoi
Springfield
New Brighton
Whitecliffs
Christchurch
Waimakariri
Riccarton
WESTLAND TAI POUTINI
Aoraki/Mt. Cook 3724
Lincoln
Lyttelton
Methven
Banks Pen.
Southern Alps (Tiritiri o te Moana)
Staveley
Akaroa
Mount Cook
AORAKI/MT. COOK
Plains
L. Ellesmere
Little River
Haast
Rakaia
Southbridge
Westland Bight
Jackson B.
L. Tekapo
Ashburton
Okuru
Canterbury
Canterbury Bight
Fairlie
L. Pukaki
MOUNT ASPIRING
Temuka
Timaru
Mt. Aspiring 3033
Ohau
St. Andrews
Mt. Earnslaw 2819
L. Wanaka
L. Hawea
Waitaki
Waimate
Milford Sd.
Sutherland Falls
Bligh Sound
Milford Sound
Wanaka
Kurow
George Sound
Arrowtown
Tokarahi
Ngapara
Queenstown
Cromwell
Dunstan Mts.
Oamaru
Secretary I.
Doubtful Sd.
Wakatipu
Naseby
Kakanui Mts.
Clyde
Alexandra
Hampden
L. Te Anau
Kingston
Otago
Dunback
FIORDLAND
Manapouri
Garvie Mts.
Umbrella Mts.
Roxburgh
Waikouaiti
Palmerston
Breaksea Sd.
Mossburn
Eyre Mts.
Port Chalmers
Otago Harbour
Resolution I.
Lumsden
Edievale
L. Mahinerangi
Dusky Sd.
Southland
Kelso
Tapanui
Dunedin
Ohai
Nightcaps
Lawrence
Mosgiel
C. Saunders
Clifden
Winton
Clinton
Milton
Chalky Inlet
Tuatapere
Hedgehope
Gore
Balclutha
Preservation Inlet
Te Waewae B.
Riverton
Mataura
Wyndham
Kaitangata
Orepuki
Invercargill
Nugget Pt.
Owaka
Solander I.
South Invercargill
Catlins
Tahakopa
Bluff
Foveaux Str.
Halfmoon Bay
Ruapuke I.
Stewart I. (Rakiura)
RAKIURA
Port Pegasus
South West C.

TAHITI & MOOREA d
1:1 000 000

Pte. Aroa
Papetoai
Paopao
Mt. Tohiea 1207
Afareaitu
Haapiti
Pte. Nuupere
Moorea (France)
PACIFIC OCEAN
B. de Matavai
Pte. Vénus
Mahina
Arue
Papenoo
Papeete
Pirae
Tiarei
Faaa
Tahiti (France)
Hitiaa
Mt. Aorai 2060
Mt. Orohena 2241
Punaauia
Faaone
Mt. Tetufera 1799
Lac Vaihiria
Isthme de Taravao
Paea
Taravao
Afaahiti
Pte. Tatatua
Maraa
Papara
Pueu
Tautira
Atimaono
Mataiea
Vairao
Mt. Roonui 1332
Teahupoo
Presqu'île de Taiarapu
17°30'
17°45'
149°45'
149°30'
149°15'
West from Greenwich

10 0 10 km
10 0 10 miles
1:1 000 000

Projection : Conical with two standard parallels
166 168 170 East from Greenwich 172

A B C D E
1 2 3 4

0
200 600
2000 6000
4000 12 000
6000 18 000
m ft

PACIFIC OCEAN

Equatorial Scale 1:54 000 000

RUSSIA
Yekaterinburg
Moskva
Volga
Tomsk
Novosibirsk
Ob
Irkutsk
Lena
Oz. Baykal
Chita
Astana
Semey
KAZAKHSTAN
Balqash Köl
Aral Sea
Almaty
Toshkent
KYRGYZSTAN
TAJIKISTAN
AFGHANISTAN
Kabul
PAKISTAN
Lahore
Delhi
Kanpur
Ürümqi
Altai
MONGOLIA
Ulaanbaatar
Blagoveshchensk
Amur
Khabarovsk
Harbin
Changchun
Shenyang
Beijing
Tianjin
Taiyuan
Huang He
Dalian
NORTH KOREA
SOUTH KOREA
Seoul
Qingdao
Lanzhou
Xi'an
CHINA
Kunlun Shan
XIZANG
Srinagar
Himalaya
Lhasa
NEPAL
Everest 8848
Ganga
Brahmaputra
BANGLADESH
Dhaka
Kolkata (Calcutta)
INDIA
Mandalay
MYANMAR
Naypyidaw
Irrawaddy
Salween
Yangôn (Rangoon)
Bay of Bengal
Hyderabad
Chennai (Madras)
Andaman Is. (India)
Nicobar Is. (India)
SRI LANKA
Colombo
LAOS
Hanoi
Hainan
Mekong
THAILAND
Bangkok
CAMBODIA
Phnom Penh
VIETNAM
Thanh Pho Ho Chi Minh
G. of Thailand
Nanjing
Wuhan
Chongqing
Chang Jiang
Changsha
Hangzhou
Shanghai
East China Sea
Fuzhou
Taipei
TAIWAN
Guangzhou
Hong Kong
Macau
Okinawa
Ryūkyū-retto (Japan)
Kitakyūshū
Yellow Sea
Kyūshū
Shikoku
Osaka
Nagoya
Kyōto
Fuji-San 3776
Tōkyō
Yokohama
JAPAN
Sendai
Sea of Japan
Sapporo
Hakodate
Vladivostok
La Perouse Str.
Sakhalin
Sea of Okhotsk
Okhotsk
Poluostrov Kamchatka
Petropavlovsk-Kamchatskiy
Kurilskiye Ostrova (Russia)
Kuril-Kamchatka Trench
10,542
Komandorskiye Ostrova (Russia)
Shirshov Ridge
Aleutian Basin
Near Is. (U.S.A.)
Andreanof Is. (U.S.A.)
7822
Aleutian Trench
Emperor Trough
Emperor Seamount Chain
Chinook
North west Pacific Basin
Shatsky Rise
Midway Is (U.S.A.)
Lisianski I. (U.S.A.)
Izu-Ogasawara Trench
10,554
Japan Trench
Ogasawara Gunto (Japan)
Iwo-Jima (Japan)
Kazan-Rettō (Japan)
Minami-Tori-Shima (Japan)
Kyushu-Palau Ridge
Shichito-Iwojima Ridge
Philippine Sea
Philippine Basin
West Mariana Basin
NORTHERN MARIANAS (U.S.A.)
Saipan
Tinian
East Mariana Basin
GUAM (U.S.A.)
Challenger Deep 11,022
Mariana Trench
Mid-Pacific Mountains
Wake I. (U.S.A.)
International Date Line
MARSHALL IS.
Bikini Atoll
Enewetak Atoll
Kwajalein
Ralik Chain
Ratak Chain
Majuro
Jaluit I.
Micronesia
Caroline Is.
Yap
Chuuk
FED. STATES OF MICRONESIA
Pohnpei
Palikir
East Caroline Basin
PALAU
Ngerulmud
West Caroline Basin
Eauripik Rise
Melanesia
Solomon Rise
Melanesian Basin
Butaritari
Tarawa
Banaba
Gilbert Is.
NAURU
Howland Baker
Phoenix Is.
Abariringa
Enderbury
KIRIBATI
Central Pacific Basin
PACIFIC OCEAN
C. Engano
Luzon
Manila
Paracel Is.
PHILIPPINES
Mindoro
Samar
10,497
Palawan
South China Sea
Sulu Sea
Mindanao
Davao
Mindanao Trench
Celebes Sea
MALAYSIA
Kuala Lumpur
PEN. MALAYSIA
Singapore
BRUNEI
SABAH
SARAWAK
4101
Borneo
Nusantara
Sumatera
Palembang
Sunda Islands
Java Sea
Jakarta
Jawa
Surabaya
Selat Sunda
Java Trench
Bali
Sumbawa
Sumba
Flores
Flores Sea
Dili
TIMOR-LESTE
Timor
Banda Sea
7440
Makassar
Sulawesi
Buru
Seram
Halmahera
Maluku
INDONESIA
Puncak Jaya 4884
PAPUA
New Guinea
PAPUA NEW GUINEA
Admiralty Is.
Bismarck Arch.
New Ireland
Kokopo
New Britain
8940
Bougainville
Lae
Port Moresby
Louisiade Arch.
SOLOMON IS.
Honiara
Guadalcanal
Santa Cruz I.
9165
Torres Strait
C. York
Arafura Sea
Fongafale
TUVALU
Tokelau (N.Z.)
Rotuma
Îs. Wallis & Futuna (Fr.)
SAMOA
Espiritu Santo
VANUATU
Port Vila
Vanua Levu
Viti Levu
Suva
FIJI
West Fiji Basin
Nuku'alofa
TONGA
Tonga Trench
10,822
Îs. Chesterfield
NEW CALEDONIA (Fr.)
Nouméa
7570
Îs. Loyauté
Coral Sea Basin
Coral Sea
Great Barrier Reef
Cairns
Townsville
Rockhampton
Great Dividing Ra.
Darwin
C. Arnhem
Gulf of Carpentaria
North Australian Basin
Exmouth Plateau
Broome
North West C.
Mount Isa
AUSTRALIA
Alice Springs
Kati Thanda-Lake Eyre
Darling
Middleton
Brisbane
Basin
Lord Howe I. (Austral.)
Lord Howe Rise
New Caledonia Trough
Norfolk I. (Austral.)
Norfolk Ridge
South Fiji Basin
Kermadec Is. (N.Z.)
Kermadec Trench
10,047
Geraldton
Perth Basin
Perth
Naturaliste Plateau
Albany
Great Australian Bight
Adelaide
Murray
Sydney
Canberra
Mt. Kosciuszko 2228
Melbourne
South Australian Basin
Bass Str.
Tasmania
Hobart
East Tasman Plateau
South Tasman Rise
Tasman Sea
Tasman Basin
NEW ZEALAND
Auckland
Cook Strait
Wellington
Chatham Rise
Chatham Is. (N.Z.)
Christchurch
Aoraki/Mt. Cook 3724
Dunedin
Bounty Trough
Bounty Is. (N.Z.)
Invercargill
Antipodes Is. (N.Z.)
Campbell Plateau
Auckland Is. (N.Z.)
Campbell I. (N.Z.)
Macquarie I. (Austral.)
Cocos Is. (Austral.)
Christmas I. (Austral.)
Ninety East Ridge
INDIAN OCEAN
Wharton Basin
Broken Ridge
Mid-Indian Ridge
Nouvelle Amsterdam (Fr.)
Î. St. Paul (Fr.)
Îs. Crozet (Fr.)
Kerguelen (Fr.)
Heard I. (Austral.)
SOUTHERN OCEAN

ft	m
12 000	4000
9000	3000
6000	2000
3000	1000
1500	500
600	200
0	0
200	600
1000	3000
2000	6000
4000	12 000
6000	18 000
8000	24 000
m	ft

Projection: Mollweide's Homolographic
East from Greenwich

ALASKA
(U.S.A.)
Anchorage
Gulf of Alaska
Prince of Wales I.
Haida Gwaii
(Queen Charlotte Is.)
Vancouver I.
Vancouver
Victoria
Seattle
Portland
C A N A D A
Edmonton
Calgary
Regina
Winnipeg
Newfoundland
Québec
Montréal
Ottawa
Toronto
Boston
New York
Philadelphia
Baltimore
Washington D.C.
UNITED STATES
San Francisco
Sacramento
Los Angeles
San Diego
Salt Lake City
Denver
Kansas City
Chicago
Detroit
Pittsburgh
Cincinnati
St. Louis
Memphis
Atlanta
Phoenix
Dallas
Houston
San Antonio
New Orleans
Jacksonville
Tampa
Miami
Gulf of Mexico
A T L A N T I C
O C E A N
Sargasso Sea
THE BAHAMAS
La Habana
CUBA
West Indies
Mexico
Puebla
Guadalajara
Monterrey
Acapulco
Caribbean Sea
Kingston
JAMAICA
HAITI
DOMINICAN REP.
Leeward Is.
Windward Is.
GUATEMALA
HONDURAS
NICARAGUA
EL SALVADOR
COSTA RICA
PANAMA
Panamá
Managua
San José
Barranquilla
Maracaibo
Caracas
VENEZUELA
COLOMBIA
Bogotá
Medellín
Cali
Quito
ECUADOR
Guayaquil
BRAZIL
PERU
Lima
Cusco
Arequipa
La Paz
BOLIVIA
PARAGUAY
Asunción
San Miguel de Tucumán
Córdoba
Rosario
Buenos Aires
Montevideo
URUGUAY
ARGENTINA
Santiago
Valparaíso
Concepción
ATLANTIC OCEAN
Falkland Is.
South Georgia
Tierra del Fuego
Drake Passage
Punta Arenas
C. de Hornos
Honolulu
HAWAIIAN IS.
Hawaii
P A C I F I C
O C E A N
Tropic of Cancer
Equator
Tropic of Capricorn
FRENCH POLYNESIA
Tahiti
Papeete
Îs. Marquises
Îs. Tuamotu
Îs. Gambier
Îs. Tubuai
Pitcairn I.
Ducie I.
Cook Is.
Rarotonga
Kiritimati
Jarvis I.
Malden I.
Starbuck I.
Î. Clipperton
Galápagos
East Pacific Ridge
Peru Basin
Chile Rise
Pacific-Antarctic Ridge
Southwest Pacific Basin
Southeast Pacific Basin
Northeast Pacific Basin
Clipperton Fracture Zone
Clarion Fracture Zone
Molokai Fracture Zone
Murray Fracture Zone
Mendocino Fracture Zone
Galápagos Fracture Zone
Marquesas Fracture Zone
Easter Fracture Zone
Challenger Fracture Zone
Menard Fracture Zone
Nasca Ridge
I. de Pascua
(Chile)
Sala-y-Gómez
Arch. de Juan Fernández
West from Greenwich

1:15 000 000

37

40

NORTHERN CANADA
Continuation northwards on same scale as main map
ARCTIC OCEAN
Sverdrup Islands
Parry Islands
Queen Elizabeth Is.
Ellesmere Island
Axel Heiberg I.
Eureka
Alert
C. Columbia
Grise Fiord
Devon Island
Lancaster Sound
Banks Island
Victoria Island
Melville I.
Prince Patrick I.
Borden I.
Brock I.
Mackenzie King I.
Ellef Ringnes I.
Amund Ringnes I.
Cornwall I.
Bathurst I.
Resolute
Prince of Wales Island
Somerset Island
Viscount Melville Sound
M'Clure Strait
M'Clintock Channel
Prince Albert Pen.
Holman
NORTHWEST TERRITORIES
NUNAVUT
Arctic Bay
Nanisivik
Brodeur Peninsula
Bylot I.
Pond Inlet
Baffin Island
GREENLAND (Denmark)
Baffin Bay
Clyde River
Qikiqtarjuaq
Cumberland Peninsula
Pangnirtung
Cumberland Sd.
Iqaluit
Frobisher Bay
Hall Peninsula
Resolution I.
Foxe Basin
Foxe Channel
Foxe Pen.
Cape Dorset
Melville Peninsula
Igloolik
Hall Beach
Prince Charles I.
Southampton I.
Coral Harbour
Repulse Bay
Hudson Strait
Hudson Bay
Salluit
Ivujivik
Kangiqsujuaq
Quaqtaq
Péninsule d'Ungava
Ungava Bay
Kangirsuk
Kuujjuaq
Akpatok I.
Puvirnituq
Inukjuak
Labrador Sea
ATLANTIC OCEAN
Hebron
Nain
Hopedale
Cartwright
NEWFOUNDLAND & LABRADOR
Labrador City
Churchill Falls
Goose Bay
Happy Valley
North West River
Smallwood Res.
Schefferville
Fermont
Belle Isle
St. Anthony
Newfoundland
Corner Brook
Gander
Bonavista
St. John's
Carbonear
Placentia
Channel-Port aux Basques
Stephenville
I. d'Anticosti
Gulf of St. Lawrence
Cabot Str.
ST.-PIERRE ET MIQUELON (Fr.)
QUÉBEC
James Bay
Chisasibi
Wemindji
Eastmain
Waskaganish
Moosonee
Attawapiskat
Fort Albany
ONTARIO
L. Mistassini
Chibougamau
Sept-Îles
Port-Cartier
Baie-Comeau
Chicoutimi
Jonquière
Québec
Trois-Rivières
Sherbrooke
MONTRÉAL
OTTAWA
Hull
Val-d'Or
Rouyn-Noranda
Timmins
Sudbury
North Bay
Sault Ste. Marie
Thunder Bay
Lake Superior
Lake Huron
Georgian Bay
TORONTO
Hamilton
Kitchener
London
Windsor
DETROIT
CHICAGO
Lake Michigan
L. Ontario
L. Erie
Buffalo
Rochester
Syracuse
CLEVELAND
Toledo
NEW YORK
BOSTON
PROVIDENCE
Hartford
New Haven
Springfield
Albany
MAINE
VERMONT
NEW HAMPSHIRE
NEW YORK
PENNSYLVANIA
NEW BRUNSWICK
Fredericton
Saint John
Moncton
Bathurst
PR. EDWARD I.
Charlottetown
Summerside
NOVA SCOTIA
Halifax
Dartmouth
Sydney
Yarmouth
Sable I.
Gaspé
Îs. de la Madeleine
Cape Breton I.
Rimouski
Matane
Labrador Sea
West from Greenwich

50 0 50 100 150 200 250 300 km

1:6 700 000

50 0 50 100 150 200 miles

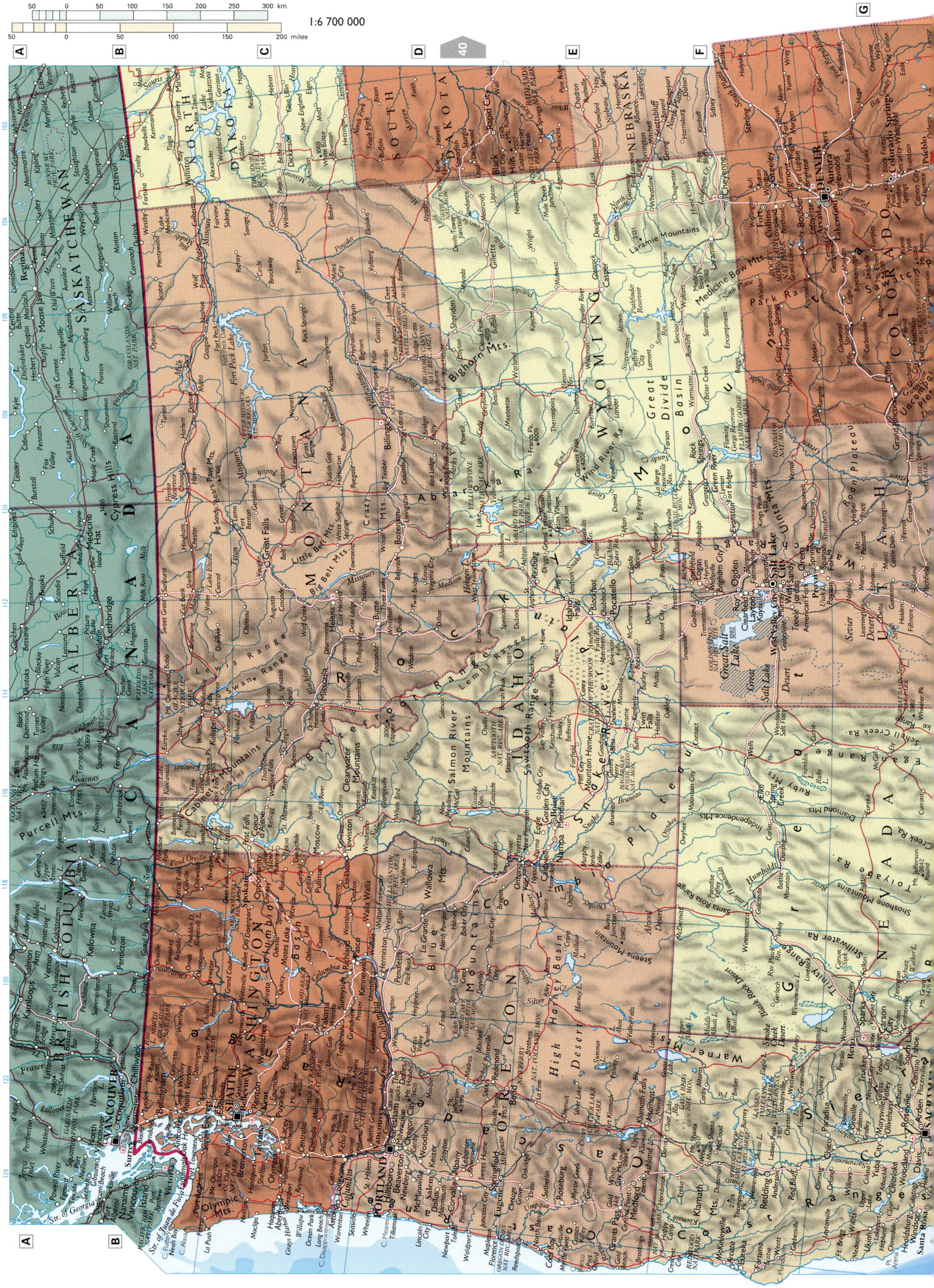

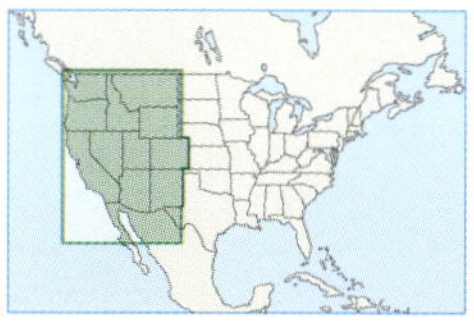

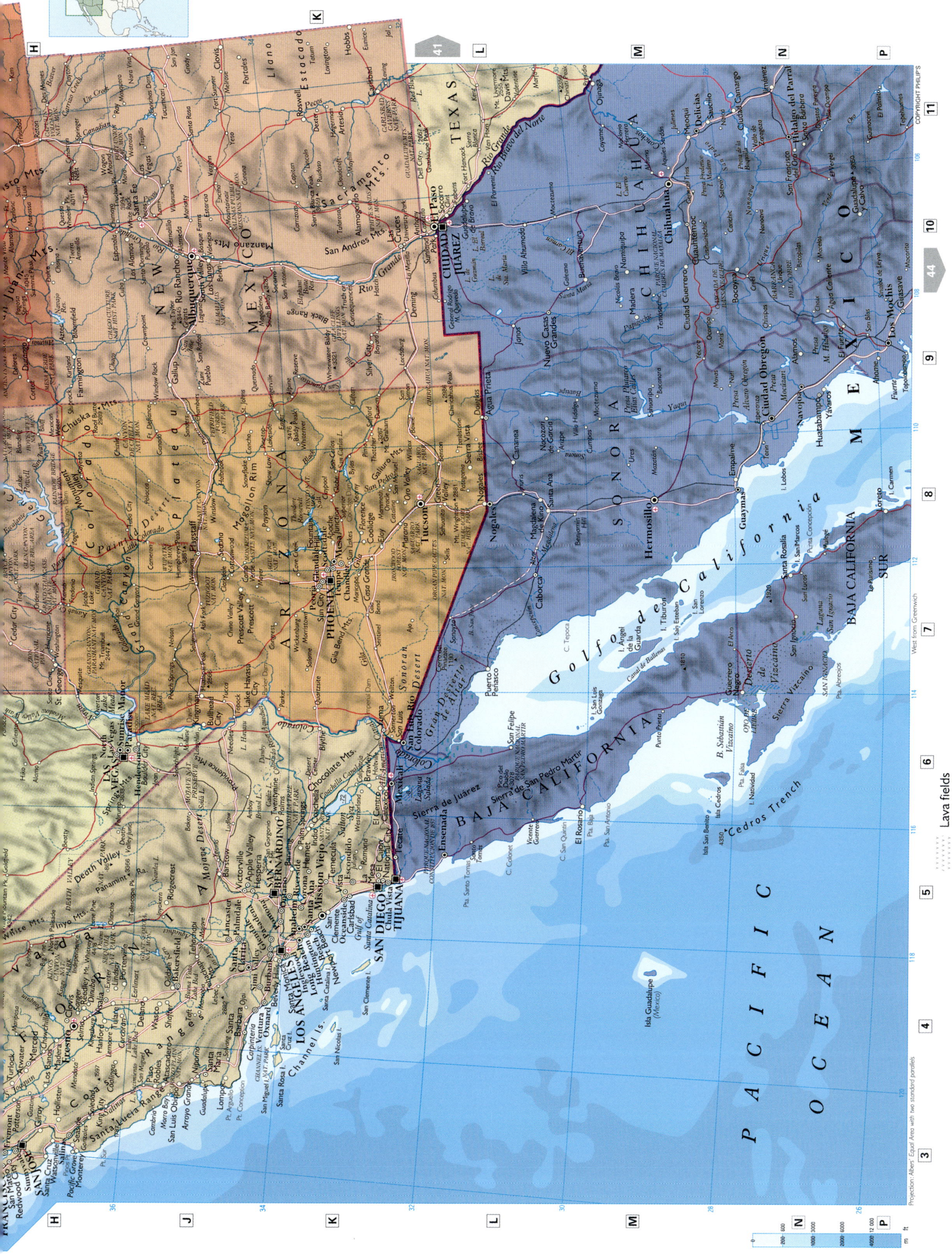

NEW MEXICO
ARIZONA
TEXAS
CHIHUAHUA
SONORA
MEXICO
BAJA CALIFORNIA
BAJA CALIFORNIA SUR
PACIFIC OCEAN
Golfo de California
Colorado Plateau
Grand Canyon
Painted Desert
Mogollon Rim
Mojave Desert
Sonoran Desert
Gran Desierto de Altar
Desierto de Vizcaíno
Llano Estacado
Sacramento Mts.
San Andres Mts.
Chocolate Mts.
Cedros Trench
Channel Is.
PHOENIX
Tucson
Albuquerque
Santa Fe
El Paso
CIUDAD JUÁREZ
Chihuahua
Hermosillo
LOS ANGELES
SAN DIEGO
TIJUANA
Mexicali
Ensenada
LAS VEGAS
SAN JOSE
Fresno
Bakersfield
Flagstaff
Yuma
Nogales
Guaymas
Ciudad Obregón
Los Mochis
Santa Rosalía
Loreto
Isla Guadalupe (Mexico)
Rio Grande
Rio Bravo del Norte
Colorado
Lava fields
West from Greenwich
Projection: Albers' Equal Area with two standard parallels
COPYRIGHT PHILIP'S

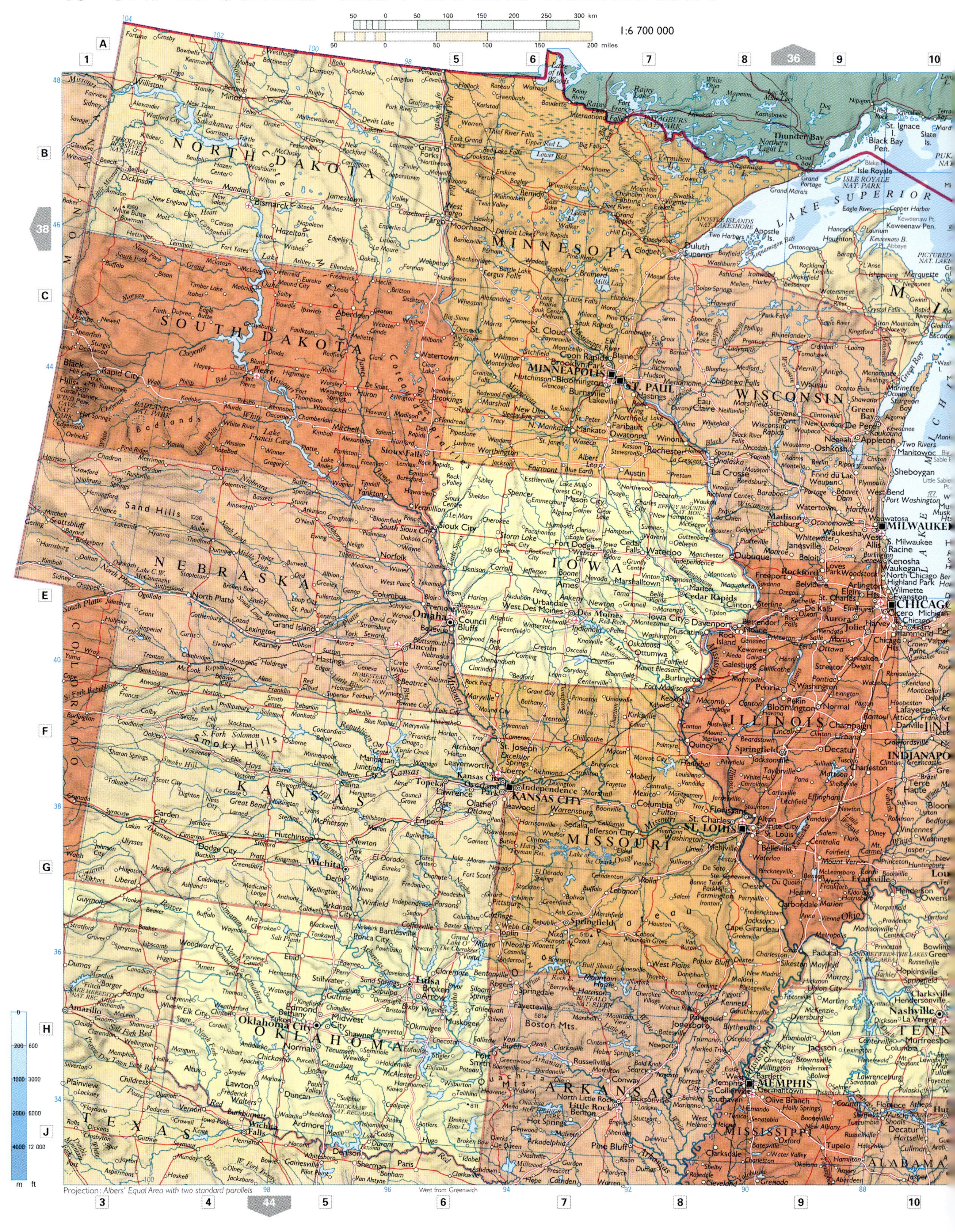
1:6 700 000
NORTH DAKOTA
SOUTH DAKOTA
NEBRASKA
KANSAS
OKLAHOMA
MINNESOTA
IOWA
MISSOURI
ARKANSAS
WISCONSIN
ILLINOIS
LAKE SUPERIOR
Projection: Albers' Equal Area with two standard parallels
West from Greenwich

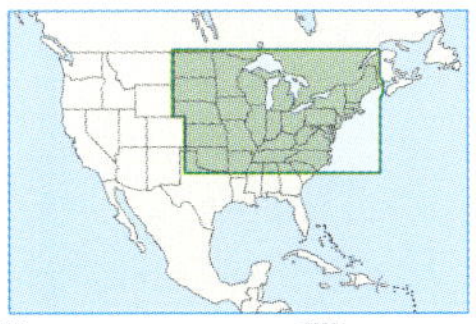

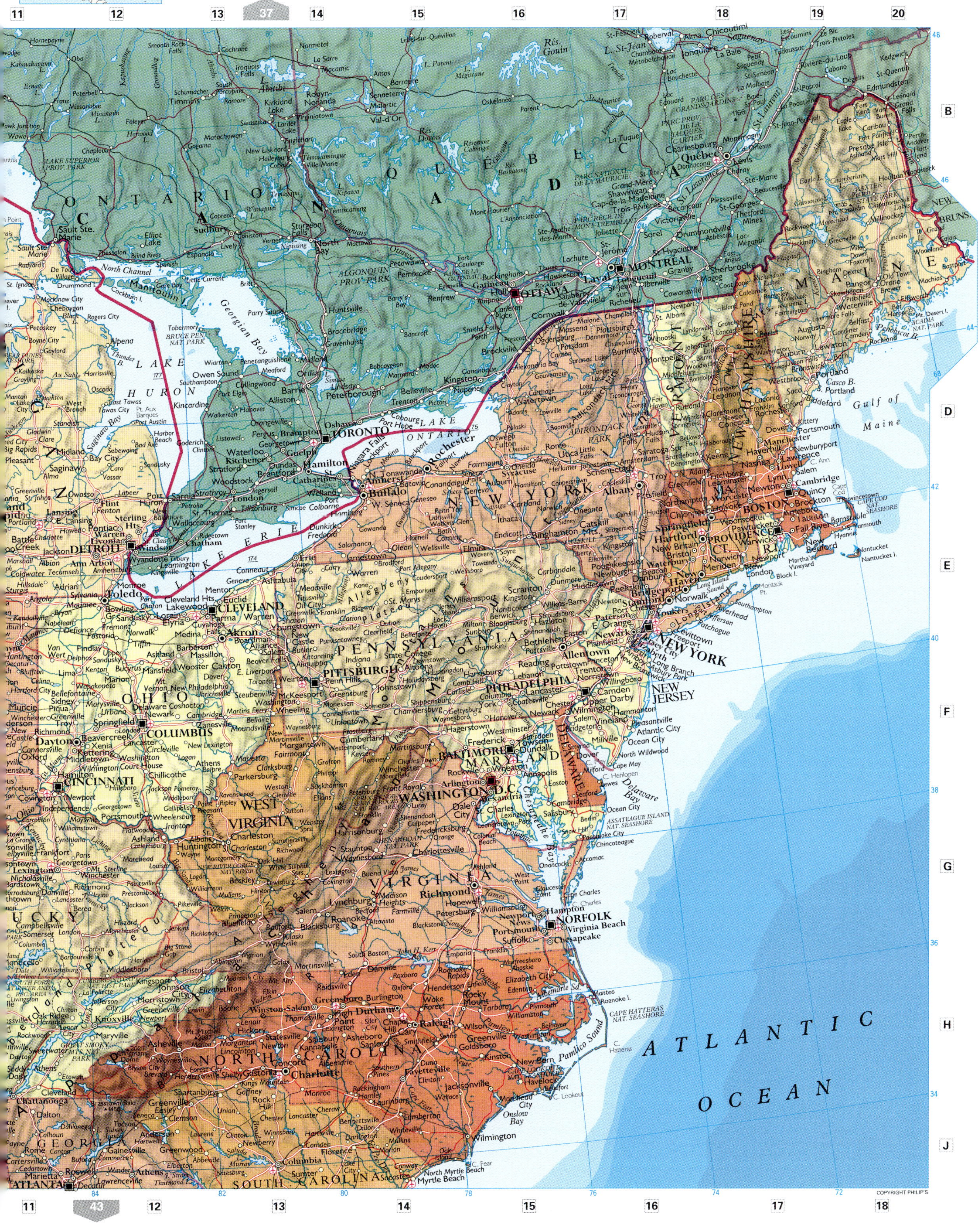

11 12 13 37 14 15 16 17 18 19 20
B
D
E
F
G
H
J
11 43 12 13 14 15 16 17 18
O N T A R I O
Q U E B E C
C A N A D A
LAKE HURON
Georgian Bay
LAKE ONTARIO
LAKE ERIE
Gulf of Maine
ATLANTIC OCEAN
NEW YORK
PENNSYLVANIA
OHIO
WEST VIRGINIA
VIRGINIA
NORTH CAROLINA
SOUTH CAROLINA
MARYLAND
DELAWARE
NEW JERSEY
VERMONT
NEW HAMPSHIRE
MAINE
MA.
CT.
R.I.
NEW BRUNS.
OTTAWA
MONTREAL
Québec
TORONTO
Hamilton
Buffalo
Rochester
Syracuse
Albany
BOSTON
PROVIDENCE
Hartford
New Haven
NEW YORK
PHILADELPHIA
PITTSBURGH
CLEVELAND
Akron
Toledo
DETROIT
COLUMBUS
Dayton
CINCINNATI
BALTIMORE
WASHINGTON D.C.
Richmond
NORFOLK
Virginia Beach
Charlotte
Raleigh
Wilmington
ATLANTA
Knoxville
Lansing
Flint
Saginaw
Windsor
London
Kingston
Sudbury
North Bay
Sault Ste. Marie
Portland
Bangor
Augusta
Manchester
Springfield
Worcester
Scranton
Allentown
Harrisburg
Charleston
Roanoke
Greensboro
Winston-Salem
Durham
Chesapeake Bay
Delaware Bay
Pamlico Sound
Cape Cod
Nantucket I.
Long Island
COPYRIGHT PHILIP'S

1:6 700 000

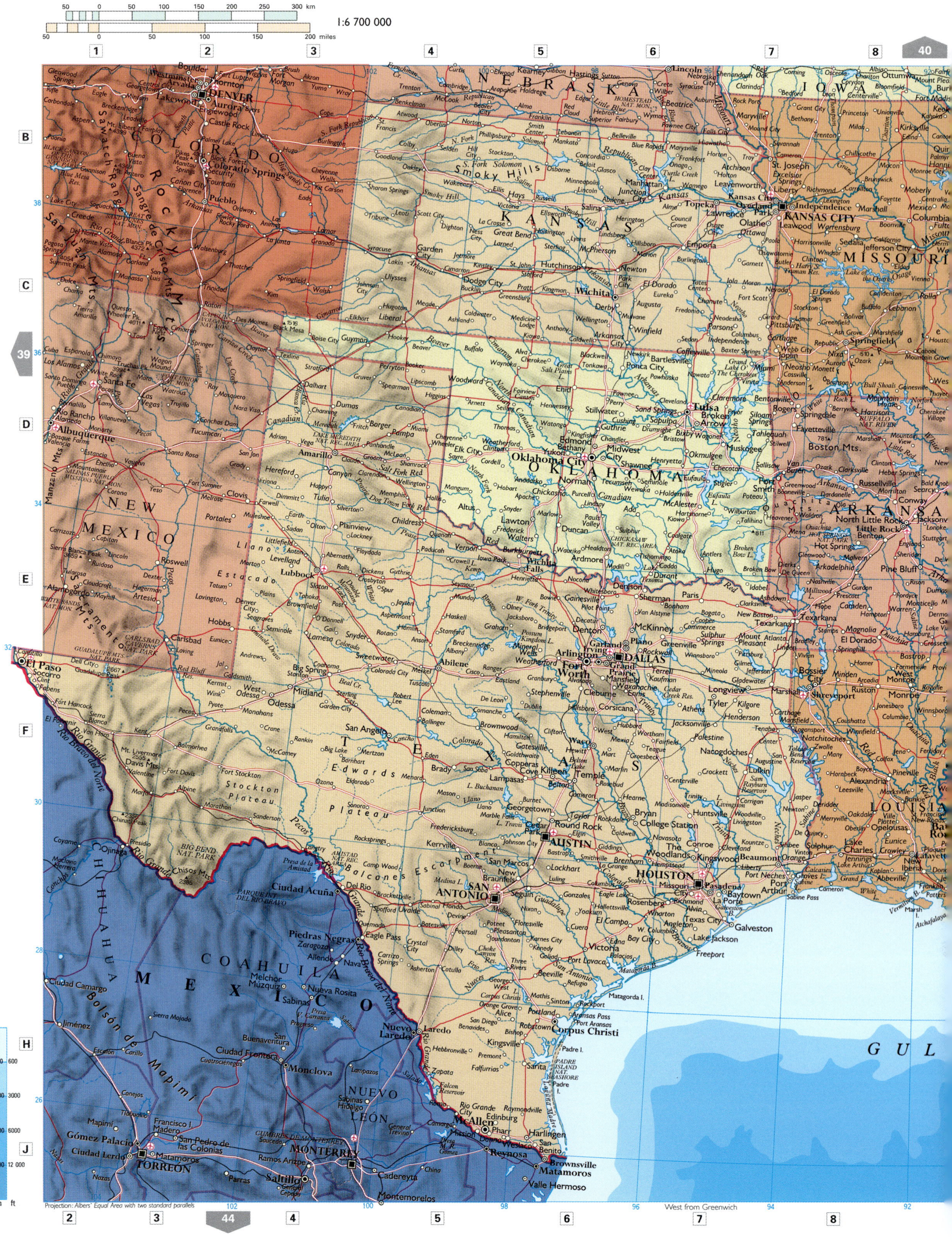

ILLINOIS
INDIANA
OHIO
PENNSYLVANIA
MARYLAND
DELAWARE
WEST VIRGINIA
VIRGINIA
KENTUCKY
TENNESSEE
NORTH CAROLINA
SOUTH CAROLINA
GEORGIA
ALABAMA
MISSISSIPPI
FLORIDA
THE BAHAMAS
ATLANTIC OCEAN
GULF OF MEXICO
INDIANAPOLIS
COLUMBUS
CINCINNATI
PITTSBURGH
PHILADELPHIA
BALTIMORE
WASHINGTON D.C.
NORFOLK
Richmond
Louisville
Nashville
MEMPHIS
ATLANTA
Birmingham
Montgomery
Charlotte
Raleigh
Columbia
Charleston
Savannah
Jacksonville
Tallahassee
ORLANDO
TAMPA
St. Petersburg
MIAMI
NEW ORLEANS
Mississippi River Delta
Florida Keys
Florida Bay
Key West
Nassau
Grand Bahama
Abaco
Andros
New Providence

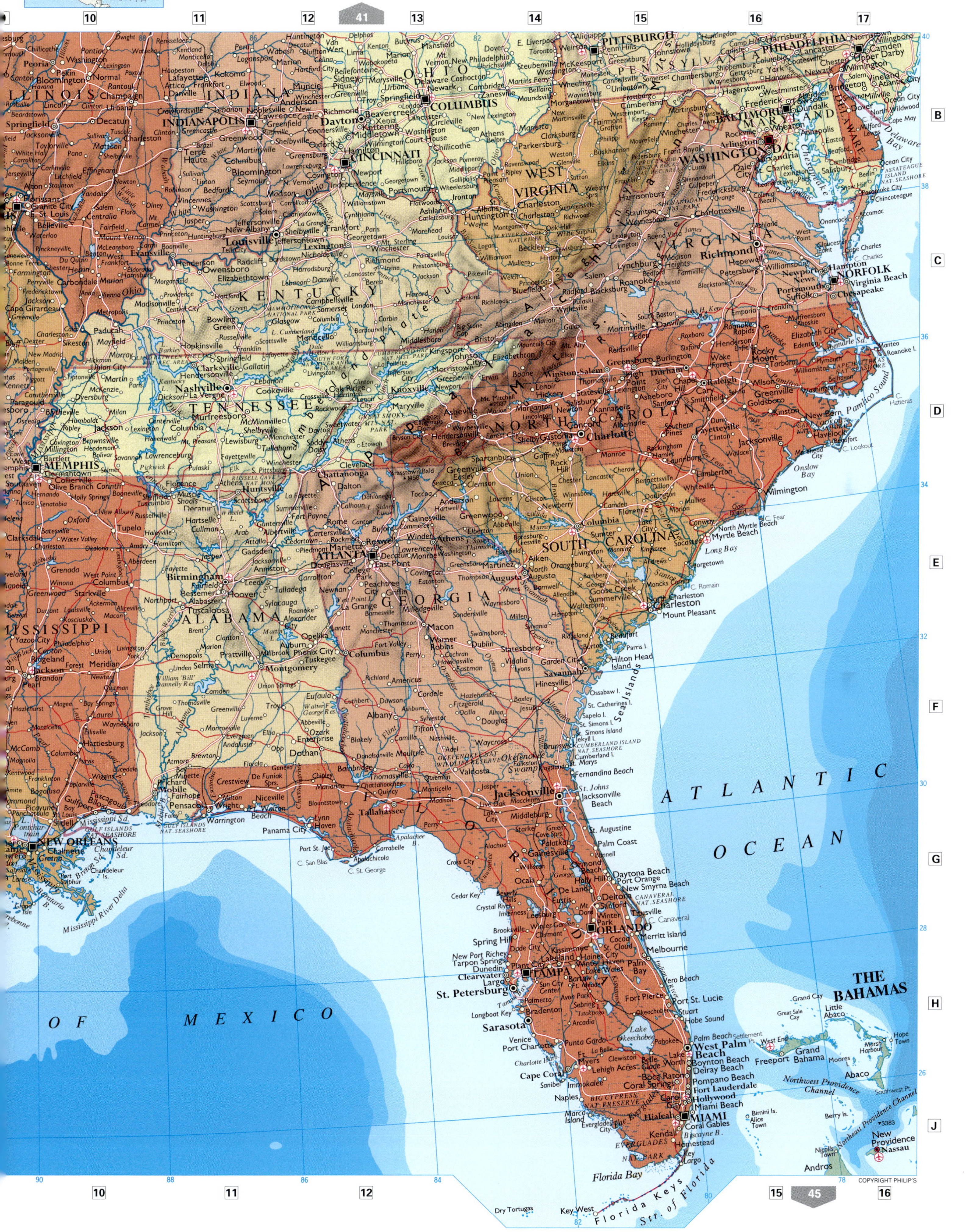

41
45

1:15 000 000

Projection : Bonne

8 9 43

PUERTO RICO d

1:3 000 000

10 0 10 20 30 40 50 km

10 0 10 20 30 miles

ATLANTIC OCEAN

PUERTO RICO (U.S.A.)

Pta. Agujereada, Aguadilla, Isabela, Arecibo, Barceloneta, Manatí, Vega Baja, Bayamón, SAN JUAN, Rio Grande, Carolina, Sierra de Luquillo, Fajardo, Dewey, Pta. Culebra, Puerca, Vieques, Esperanza, Mayagüez, San Sebastián, Utuado, Adjuntas, Cordillera Central, C. de Punta 1338, Uroyan Mts., Caguas, Cayey, Humacao, Naguabo, San Germán, Yauco, Coamo, Yabucoa, Ponce, Guayama, Pta. Aguila, Guanica, I. Caja de Muertos

VIRGIN IS. e

1:2 000 000

10 0 10 20 30 km

10 0 10 20 miles

Virgin Islands (U.K.)

The Settlement, Rufling Pt., Anegada, East Pt., Great Camanoe, Jost Van Dyke I., Guana I., Beef I., Virgin Gorda, Spanish Town, Virgin Is. (U.S.A.), Hans Lollik I., Tortola 521, Road Town, Cruz Bay, Peter I., Charlotte Amalie, St. Thomas I., St. John I.

ST. LUCIA f

1:1 000 000

5 0 10 km

5 0 5 10 miles

Cap Point, Pte. Hardy, Gros Islet, Esperance Bay, Castries, Marquis, Girard, Anse la Raye, Canaries, Millet, Dennery, Mt. Gimie 950, Soufrière, Soufrière Bay, Petit Piton 750, Gros Piton 798, Trou Gras Pt., Micoud, Vierge Pt., Gros Piton Pt., Choiseul, ST. LUCIA, Laborie, Vieux Fort, C. Moule à Chique

BARBADOS g

1:1 000 000

5 0 10 km

5 0 5 10 miles

ATLANTIC OCEAN

North Point, Crab Hill, Spring Hall, Fustic, Boscobelle, Belleplaine 245, BARBADOS, Speightstown, Westmoreland, Bathsheba, Hillcrest, Alleynes Bay, Mt. Hillaby 340, Martin's Bay, Holetown, Jackson, Bridgefield, Massiah Street, Kitridge Pt., Black Rock, Ellerton, Six Cross Roads, The Crane, Bridgetown, Carlisle Bay, Oistins, St. Martins, Worthing, Oistins Bay, Chancery Lane, South Point

Main map

Wilmington, C. Fear, Long Bay, C. Romain, Charleston, Columbia, Augusta, Savannah, Macon, Jacksonville, Daytona Beach, ORLANDO, C. Canaveral, Melbourne, St. Petersburg, West Palm Beach, L. Okeechobee, Fort Lauderdale, MIAMI, C. Sable, Key West, Straits of Florida

Grand Bahama, Freeport, Abaco, Bimini, New Providence, Eleuthera, Nassau, Andros, THE BAHAMAS, Cat I., San Salvador, Great Exuma, Long I., Crooked I., Mayaguana I., Acklins, Great Inagua I., Turks & Caicos Is., Cockburn Town (U.K.)

HABANA (Havana), Matanzas, Cárdenas, Sagua la Grande, Santa Clara, G. de Batabanó, Güines, CUBA, Cienfuegos, Placetas, Morón, Camagüey, Nuevitas, Trinidad, Sancti Spíritus, Ciego de Avila, Holguín, Las Tunas, Banes, I. de la Juventud, Manzanillo, Bayamo, Santiago de Cuba, Guantánamo, Baracoa, GUANTANAMO (U.S.A.), 1972

Greater Antilles, Cayman Is., Grand Cayman, George Town (U.K.), 7680, Montego Bay, Mandeville, JAMAICA, Spanish Town, Kingston

Windward Passage, Port-de-Paix, Cap-Haïtien, Monte Cristi, Puerto Plata, Santiago de los Caballeros, San Francisco de Macorís, HAITI, Gonaïves, St-Marc, Jérémie, Les Cayes, Jacmel, PORT-AU-PRINCE, 3175, DOMINICAN REP., La Vega, San Juan, Barahona, Baní, La Romana, San Pedro de Macorís, SANTO DOMINGO, Hispaniola, Puerto Rico Trench, 8605, Mona Passage, Mona, Arecibo, SAN JUAN, Caguas, Ponce, Mayagüez, PUERTO RICO (U.S.A.), St. Croix (U.S.A.), Virgin Is. (U.S.A. - U.K.)

Anguilla (U.K.), St-Martin (Fr. - Neth.), St-Barthélemy (Fr.), ST. KITTS & NEVIS, Basseterre, ANTIGUA & BARBUDA, St. John's, Montserrat (U.K.), GUADELOUPE (Fr.), Pointe-à-Pitre, Basse-Terre, Leeward Islands, DOMINICA, Roseau, Lesser Antilles, Fort-de-France, MARTINIQUE (Fr.), Castries, ST. LUCIA, ST. VINCENT & THE GRENADINES, Kingstown, Bridgetown, BARBADOS, Windward Islands, GRENADA, St. George's, Tobago, TRINIDAD & TOBAGO, Port of Spain, San Fernando

CARIBBEAN SEA

L. de Caratasca, C. Gracias a Dios, Puerto Cabezas, I. de Providencia (Colombia), Río Grande, I. de San Andrés (Colombia), Bluefields, COSTA RICA, Irazú 3432, Limón, Cartago, G. de los Mosquitos, Panama Canal, Colón, Volcan Barú 3475, David, PANAMA, Panamá, Santiago, Chitré, Pen. de Azuero, I. de Coiba, Arch. de las Perlas, G. de Panamá, La Palma, El Real, G. del Darién, I. de Malpelo (Colombia)

Pen. de la Guajira, Pta. Gallinas, Riohacha, Santa Marta, Sierra Nevada de Santa Marta 5800, BARRANQUILLA, Soledad, Cartagena, Calamar, Valledupar, Sincelejo, Montería, Mompós, Magdalena, Cauca, Cúcuta, Puerto Wilches, Barrancabermeja, Yarumal, Riosucio, 3960, Bucaramanga, Pamplona, Antioquia, Bello, MEDELLÍN, Quibdó, G. de Cupica, C. Corrientes, Sogamosa, Tunja, Manizales, Pereira, Armenia, Tolima 5215, Ibagué, BOGOTÁ, Girardot, Villavicencio, Buenaventura, Palmira, CALI, Huila 5750, Neiva, Popayán, Volcan Puracé 4646, COLOMBIA, Meta, Vichada, Guaviare, Puerto Inírida

G. de Venezuela, Aruba, Curaçao, Willemstad, Bonaire, ABC Islands (Neth.), Punto Fijo, Coro, MARACAIBO, San Felipe, Cabimas, L. de Maracaibo, Barquisimeto, Puerto Cabello, MARACAY, Maiquetía, CARACAS, VALENCIA, Acarigua, Valera, Mérida 5007, Barinas, Apure, San Fernando de Apure, San Cristóbal, Arauca, Puerto Carreño, Puerto Ayacucho, La Tortuga, I. de Margarita, Porlamar, Carúpano, Cumaná, Puerto La Cruz, 2596, Barcelona, El Tigre, Maturín, Tucupita, G. de Paria, Güiria, La Blanquilla (Ven.), Orinoco, Ciudad Guayana, Ciudad Bolívar, Embalse de Guri, Caicara, Caura, Caroní, Angel Falls, VENEZUELA, Ventuari, Sierra Pacaraima, Mt. Roraima 2810, Serra Parima, Boa Vista, BRAZIL, Equator

GUYANA, Georgetown, Cuyuni, Tumeremo, Essequibo, Bartica, New Amsterdam, Linden, Wismar, SURINAME

1:16 000 000

Projection: Sanson-Flamsteed's Sinusoidal

ATLANTIC OCEAN
TRINIDAD AND TOBAGO
1:2 500 000
Tobago
Trinidad
Golfo de Paria
Serpent's Mouth
VENEZUELA
Port of Spain
San Fernando
Scarborough
FRENCH GUIANA
Cayenne
AMAPÁ
Macapá
BELÉM
São Luís
MARANHÃO
Teresina
PIAUÍ
FORTALEZA
CEARÁ
Natal
João Pessoa
RECIFE
PERNAMBUCO
Maceió
ALAGOAS
Aracaju
SERGIPE
SALVADOR
BAHIA
TOCANTINS
Palmas
BRASÍLIA
GOIÂNIA
GOIÁS
MINAS GERAIS
BELO HORIZONTE
Vitória
RIO DE JANEIRO
CAMPINAS
Campo Grande
MATO GROSSO
Equator
Fernando de Noronha (Braz.)
Trindade (Braz.)
Martin Vaz
São Paulo (Braz.)
COPYRIGHT PHILIP'S

1:16 000 000
PACIFIC OCEAN
ATLANTIC OCEAN
Peru-Chile Trench
Tropic of Capricorn
PARAGUAY
ASUNCIÓN
URUGUAY
MONTEVIDEO
BUENOS AIRES
ROSARIO
CÓRDOBA
SANTIAGO
Mendoza
Valparaíso
Viña del Mar
San Miguel de Tucumán
Salta
Antofagasta
Concepción
Temuco
Valdivia
Puerto Montt
Mar del Plata
Bahía Blanca
Comodoro Rivadavia
Río Gallegos
Punta Arenas
Tierra del Fuego
Ushuaia
FALKLAND ISLANDS (ISLAS MALVINAS) (U.K.)
Stanley
West Falkland
East Falkland
South Georgia (U.K.)
Grytviken
SÃO PAULO
RIO DE JANEIRO
CURITIBA
PORTO ALEGRE
Florianópolis
CAMPINAS
SANTOS
Estrecho de Magallanes
Río de la Plata
Pen. Valdés
Golfo San Matías
Golfo San Jorge
I. de Chiloé
Arch. de los Chonos
Pen. de Taitao
I. de Los Estados (Staten I.)
C. de Hornos (C. Horn)
Projection: Sanson-Flamsteed's Sinusoidal
West from Greenwich

INDEX

The index contains the names of all the principal places and features shown on the maps. The alphabetical order of names composed of two or more words is governed primarily by the first word and then by the second. This is an example of the rule:

New York	**41**	**E17**
New York □	**41**	**D16**
New Zealand ■	**33**	**D6**
Newark, Del., U.S.A.	**41**	**F16**
Newark, N.J., U.S.A.	**41**	**E16**

Physical features composed of a proper name (Erie) and a description (Lake) are positioned alphabetically by the proper name. The description is positioned after the proper name and is usually abbreviated:

Erie, L.	**41**	**D13**
Everest, Mt.	**25**	**E13**

Where a description forms part of a settlement name or administrative name, however, it is always written in full and put in its true alphabetical position:

Lake Charles	**42**	**F8**
Mount Isa	**30**	**E6**

The number in bold type which follows each name in the index refers to the number of the map page where that place or feature will be found. This is usually the largest scale at which the place or feature appears.

The letter and figure which are immediately after the page number give the grid square on the map page, within which the feature is situated. The letter represents the latitude and the figure the longitude. In some cases the feature itself may fall within the specified square, while the name is outside.

Rivers are indexed to their mouths or confluences and carry the symbol → after their names. The following symbols are also used in the index: ■ country, ☑ overseas territory or dependency, □ first order administrative area, △ national park or ⌓ reserve.

A

A Coruña 13 A1
Aachen 16 C3
Aalborg 7 F5
Aarau 12 C8
Aare → 12 C8
Aarhus 7 F6
Aba 26 G7
Abaco 45 B9
Ābādān 24 C5
Abaetetuba 47 D9
Abakan 19 D10
Abancay 46 F4
Abariringa 31 A16
Abbaye, Pt. 40 B9
Abbeville, *France* 12 A4
Abbeville, *Ala., U.S.A.* 43 F12
Abbeville, *La., U.S.A.* 42 G8
Abbeville, *S.C., U.S.A.* 43 D13
Abbot Ice Shelf 6 E2
ABC Islands 45 E11
Abéché 27 F10
Abeokuta 26 G6
Aberaeron 9 E3
Aberchirder 10 D6
Aberdare 9 F4
Aberdeen, *China* 21 a
Aberdeen, *U.K.* 10 D6
Aberdeen, *Idaho, U.S.A.* 38 E7
Aberdeen, *Md., U.S.A.* 41 F15
Aberdeen, *Miss., U.S.A.* 43 E10
Aberdeen, *S. Dak., U.S.A.* 40 C4
Aberdeen, *Wash., U.S.A.* 38 C2
Aberdeenshire □ 10 D6
Aberdyfi 9 E3
Aberfeldy 10 E5
Aberfoyle 10 E4
Abergavenny 9 F4
Abergele 8 D4
Abernathy 42 E4
Abert, L. 38 E3
Aberystwyth 9 E3
Abhā 24 F4
Abidjan 26 G5
Abilene, *Kans., U.S.A.* 40 F5
Abilene, *Tex., U.S.A.* 42 E5
Abingdon, *U.K.* 9 F6
Abingdon, *U.S.A.* 41 G13
Abitibi, L. 37 E12
Abkhazia □ 17 B6
Abomey 26 G6
Aboyne 10 D6
Absaroka Range 38 D9
Abu Dhabi = Abū Ẓāby 24 E6
Abu Hamed 27 E12
Abū Ẓāby 24 E6
Abuja 26 G7
Abunã 46 E5
Abunã → 46 E5
Acadia △ 41 C19
Acaponeta 44 C3
Acapulco 44 D5
Acaraí, Serra 46 C7
Acarigua 46 B5
Accomac 41 G16
Accra 26 G5
Accrington 8 D5
Aceh □ 25 J15
Acharnes 15 E10
Acheloos → 15 E9
Achill Hd. 11 C1
Achill I. 11 C1
Achinsk 19 D10
Ackerman 43 E10
Acklins 45 C10
Aconcagua, Cerro 48 C3
Açores, Is. dos 26 a
Acre □ 46 E4
Acre → 46 E5
Ad Dammām 24 D6
Ad Dawḥah 24 D6
Ad Dīwānīyah 24 C5
Ada, *Minn., U.S.A.* 40 B5
Ada, *Okla., U.S.A.* 42 D6
Adair, C. 37 B12
Adak I. 36 D2
Adamaoua, Massif de l' 27 G8
Adams, *N.Y., U.S.A.* 41 D15
Adams, *Wis., U.S.A.* 40 D9
Adams, Mt. 38 C3
'Adan 24 G3
Adana 17 C5
Adare, C. 6 E15
Addis Abeba 28 C7
Adel 43 F13
Adelaide 32 B2
Adelaide I. 6 D3
Adelaide Pen. 36 C10
Adélie, Terre 6 D14
Aden = 'Adan 24 G5
Aden, G. of 24 G5
Adige → 14 B5
Adirondack △ 41 D16
Adirondack Mts. 41 D17
Adjuntas 45 d
Admiralty Is. 34 H6
Adour → 12 E3
Adrar, *Algeria* 26 C6
Adrar, *Mauritania* 26 D3
Adrar des Iforas 26 E6
Adrian, *Mich., U.S.A.* 41 E11
Adrian, *Tex., U.S.A.* 42 D3
Adriatic Sea 14 C6
Adwa 24 G3
Adygea □ 17 B6
Aegean Sea 15 E11
Aerhtai Shan 20 B7
Afghanistan ■ 24 C9
Africa 3 D11
Afton 38 E8
Afyon 17 C4
Agadez 26 E7
Agadir 26 B4
Agen 12 D4
Agra 25 D11
Ağri 17 C6
Ağrı Dağı 17 C6
Agrigento 14 F5
Agua Fria △ 39 J8
Agua Prieta 44 A3
Aguadilla 45 d
Aguascalientes 44 C4
Aguila, Punta 45 d
Agujereada, Pta. 45 d
Agulhas, C. 29 L4
Ahaggar 26 D7
Ahmadabad 25 E10
Ahmadnagar 25 F10
Ahoskie 43 C16
Ahvāz 24 C5
Ahvenanmaa = Åland 7 E8
Aiken 43 E14
Ailsa Craig 10 F3
Aïn Témouchent 26 A5
Ainsworth 40 D4
Aïr 26 E7
Air Force I. 37 C12
Airdrie, *Canada* 36 D8
Airdrie, *U.K.* 10 F5
Aire → 8 D7
Aisne → 12 B5
Aitkin 40 B7
Aix-en-Provence 12 E6
Aix-les-Bains 12 D6
Aizuwakamatsu 22 E6
Ajaccio 12 F8
Ajaria □ 17 B6
Ajdābiyā 27 B10
Ajmer 25 D10
Ajo 39 K7
Aketi 28 D4
Akhisar 15 E12
Akimiski I. 37 D11
Akita 22 D7
'Akko 17 D5
Aklavik 36 C6
Akola 25 E11
Akpatok I. 37 C13
Akranes 7 B1
Akron, *Colo., U.S.A.* 38 F12
Akron, *Ohio, U.S.A.* 41 E13
Aksai Chin 20 D4
Aksaray 17 C4
Akşehir Gölü 17 C4
Aksu 20 C5
Aksum 24 G3
Akure 26 G7
Akureyri 7 A2
Al 'Amārah 24 C5
Al 'Aqabah 24 D3
Al 'Ayn 24 E7
Al Başrah 24 C5
Al Bayḍā 27 B10
Al Ḥillah 24 C4
Al Hoceïma 26 A5
Al Ḥudaydah 24 G4
Al Hufūf 24 D5
Al Jawf, *Libya* 27 D10
Al Jawf, *Si. Arabia* 24 D3
Al Jazirah 24 C4
Al Jubayl 24 D5
Al Junaynah 27 F10
Al Khums 27 B8
Al Kufrah 27 D10
Al Kūt 24 C5
Al Kuwayt 24 D5
Al Lādhiqīyah 24 B3
Al Madīnah 24 E3
Al Manāmah 24 D6
Al Mawşil 24 B4
Al Mubarraz 24 D5
Al Mukallā 24 G5
Al Qaţīf 24 D6
Al Qunfudhah 24 F4
Ala Tau 20 B5
Alabama □ 43 E11
Alabama → 43 F11
Alabaster 43 E11
Alachua 43 G13
Alagoas □ 47 E11
Alagoinhas 47 F11
Alameda 39 J10
Alamo 39 H6
Alamogordo 39 K11
Åland 7 E8
Alanya 17 C4
Alappuzha 25 H11
Alaşehir 15 E13
Alaska □ 36 C4
Alaska, G. of 36 D5
Alaska Peninsula 36 D4
Alaska Range 36 C4
Alava, C. 38 B1
Alba-Iulia 15 A10
Albacete 13 C5
Albanel, L. 37 D12
Albania ■ 15 D9
Albany, *Australia* 30 H2
Albany, *Ga., U.S.A.* 43 F12
Albany, *N.Y., U.S.A.* 41 D17
Albany, *Oreg., U.S.A.* 38 D2
Albany, *Tex., U.S.A.* 42 E5
Albany → 37 D11
Albemarle 43 D14
Albemarle Sd. 43 C16
Albert, L. 28 D6
Albert Lea 40 D7
Albert Nile → 28 D6
Alberta □ 36 D8
Albertville, *France* 12 D7
Albertville, *U.S.A.* 43 D11
Albi 12 E5
Albia 40 E7
Albion, *Mich., U.S.A.* 41 D11
Albion, *Nebr., U.S.A.* 40 E4
Alborz, Reshteh-ye Kūhhā-ye 24 B6
Albuquerque 39 J10
Albury 32 C4
Alcalá de Henares 13 B4
Alchevsk 17 A5
Alcova 38 E10
Alcoy 13 C5
Aldabra Is. 5 E12
Aldan 19 D13
Aldan → 19 C13
Aldeburgh 9 E9
Alderney 9 H5
Aldershot 9 F7
Aledo 40 E8
Alegrete 48 B5
Alençon 12 B4
Alenquer 47 D8
Aleppo = Ḥalab 24 B3
Alert 37 A13
Alès 12 D6
Alessándria 12 D8
Ålesund 7 E5
Aleutian Is. 36 D2
Aleutian Trench 34 C10
Alexander 40 B2
Alexander Arch. 36 D6
Alexander City 43 E12
Alexander I. 6 D3
Alexandria = El Iskandarîya 27 B11
Alexandria, *U.K.* 10 F4
Alexandria, *La., U.S.A.* 42 F8
Alexandria, *Minn., U.S.A.* 40 C6
Alexandria, *S. Dak., U.S.A.* 40 D5
Alexandria, *Va., U.S.A.* 41 F15
Alexandria Bay 41 C16
Alford, *Aberds., U.K.* 10 D6
Alford, *Lincs., U.K.* 8 D8
Alfreton 8 D6
Algarve 13 D1
Algeciras 13 D3
Alger 26 A6
Algeria ■ 26 C6
Algiers = Alger 26 A6
Algoma 40 C10
Algona 40 D6
Alicante 13 C5
Alice 42 H5
Alice Springs 30 E5
Aliceville 43 E10
Aligarh 25 D11
Aliquippa 41 E13
Aliwal North 29 L5
Alkmaar 16 B2
All American Canal 39 K6
Allagash → 41 B19
Allegheny → 41 E13
Allegheny Mts. 41 F13
Allegheny Plateau 41 E14
Allègre, Pte. 44 b
Allen, Bog of 11 C5
Allen, L. 11 B3
Allendale 43 E14
Allentown 41 E16
Alleynes B. 45 g
Alliance, *Nebr., U.S.A.* 40 D2
Alliance, *Ohio, U.S.A.* 41 E13
Allier → 12 C5
Alligator Pond 44 a
Alliston 41 C14
Alloa 10 E5
Alluitsup Paa 6 C4
Alma, *Ga., U.S.A.* 43 F13
Alma, *Kans., U.S.A.* 40 F5
Alma, *Mich., U.S.A.* 41 D11
Alma, *Nebr., U.S.A.* 40 E4
Alma, *Wis., U.S.A.* 40 C8
Alma Ata = Almaty 18 E8
Almada 13 C1
Almanor, L. 38 F3
Almaty 18 E8
Almelo 16 B3
Almería 13 D4
Alness 10 D4
Alnmouth 8 B6
Alnwick 8 B6
Alor 23 D4
Alor Setar 23 C2
Alpena 41 C12
Alpine, *Ariz., U.S.A.* 39 K9
Alpine, *Tex., U.S.A.* 42 F3
Alps 14 A3
Alsace □ 12 B7
Alston 8 C5
Altai = Aerhtai Shan 20 B7
Altamaha → 43 F14
Altamira 47 D8
Altamura 14 D7
Altavista 41 G14
Altay, *China* 20 B6
Altay, *Mongolia* 20 B6
Altiplano 46 G5
Alton, *U.K.* 9 F7
Alton, *U.S.A.* 40 F9
Altoona 41 E14
Altun Shan 20 C6
Alturas 38 F3
Altus 42 D5
Alucra 17 B5
Alva 42 C5
Alvarado 42 E6
Alvin 42 G7
Alvord Desert 38 E4
Alxa Zuoqi 20 C5
Alyth 10 E5
Alzada 38 D11
Amadjuak L. 37 C12
Amagasaki 22 F4
Amapá 47 C8
Amapá □ 47 C8
Amarillo 42 D4
Amazon = Amazonas → 47 D8
Amazonas □ 46 D6
Amazonas → 47 D8
Ambala 25 C11
Ambato 46 D3
Ambergris Cay 44 D7
Ambilobé 29 G9
Amble 8 B6
Ambleside 8 C5
Ambon 23 D4
Amboy 39 J6
Amchitka I. 36 D1
Amderma 18 C7
Amdo 20 C4
Ameca 44 C4
Ameland 16 B2
American Falls 38 E7
American Falls Res. 38 E7
American Fork 38 F8
American Highland 6 E10
American Samoa ☑ 33 b
Americus 43 E12
Ames 40 E8
Amherst, *Canada* 37 E13
Amherst, *U.S.A.* 41 D14
Amiens 12 B5
Amirante Is. 5 E12
Amistad ⌓ 42 G4
Amite 43 F9
Amlia I. 36 D2
Amlwch 8 D3
'Ammān 24 C3
Ammanford 9 F4
Amory 43 E10
Amos 37 E12
Amravati 25 E11
Amritsar 25 C10
Amsterdam, *Neths.* 16 B2
Amsterdam, *U.S.A.* 41 D16
Amudarya → 24 A7
Amund Ringnes I. 37 B10
Amundsen Gulf 36 B7
Amundsen Sea 6 E1
Amuntai 23 D3
Amur → 19 D15
An Nafūd 24 D4
An Najaf 24 C4
An Nāşirīyah 24 C5
Anaconda 38 C7
Anacortes 38 B2
Anadarko 42 D5
Anadolu 17 C4
Anadyr 19 C18
Anadyrskiy Zaliv 19 C19
Anaheim 39 K5
Anambas, Kepulauan 23 C2
Anamosa 40 D8
Anamur 17 C4
Anápolis 47 G9
Anār 24 C7
Anatolia = Anadolu 17 C4
Añatuya 48 B4
Anchorage 36 C5
Anci 21 D12
Ancohuma, Nevado 46 G5
Ancona 14 C5
Ancud 48 E2
Ancud, G. de 48 E2
Anda 21 B14
Andalgalá 48 B3
Andalucía □ 13 D3
Andalusia 43 F11
Andaman Is. 25 G14
Anderson, *Alaska, U.S.A.* 36 C5
Anderson, *Calif., U.S.A.* 38 F2
Anderson, *Ind., U.S.A.* 41 E11
Anderson, *Mo., U.S.A.* 40 G6
Anderson, *S.C., U.S.A.* 43 D13
Anderson → 36 C7
Andes, Cord. de los 46 H5
Andhra Pradesh □ 25 G11
Andijon 18 E8
Andorra ■ 12 E4
Andorra La Vella 12 E4
Andover 9 F6
Andradina 47 H8
Andreanof Is. 36 D2
Andrews, *S.C., U.S.A.* 43 E15
Andrews, *Tex., U.S.A.* 42 E3
Ándria 14 D7
Andros 15 F11
Andros 45 C9
Anegada 45 e
Aneityum 31 E12
Angara → 19 D10
Angarsk 19 D11
Ånge 7 E7
Angel Falls 46 B6
Angeles 23 B4
Angels Camp 39 G3
Ångermanälven → 7 E7
Angers 12 C3
Anglesey, Isle of □ 8 D3
Angleton 42 G7
Angoche 29 H7
Angola ■ 29 G3
Angoulême 12 D4
Angoumois 12 D4
Anguilla ☑ 45 D12
Angus □ 10 E6
Anhui □ 21 E12
Animas → 39 H9
Anjou 12 C3
Ankaboa, Tanjona 29 J8
Ankang 21 E10
Ankara 17 C5
Ankeny 40 E8
Ann, C. 41 D18
Ann Arbor 41 D12
Anna 40 G9
Annaba 26 A7
Annalee → 11 B4
Annan 10 G5
Annapolis 41 F15
Annapurna 25 D12
Annecy 12 D7
Anniston 43 E12
Annotto B. 44 a
Anqing 21 E12
Anse la Raye 45 f
Anshan 21 C13
Anshun 20 F10
Ansley 40 E4
Anson 42 E5
Anstruther 10 E6
Antakya 17 C6
Antalya 17 C4
Antalya Körfezi 17 C4
Antananarivo 29 H9
Antarctic Pen. 6 D4
Antarctica 6 F7
Antero, Mt. 38 G10
Anthony, *Kans., U.S.A.* 40 G4
Anthony, *N. Mex., U.S.A.* 39 K10
Anti Atlas 26 C4
Antibes 12 E7
Anticosti, Î. d' 37 E13
Antigo 40 C9
Antigonish 37 E13
Antigua & Barbuda ■ 45 D12
Antioquia 46 B3
Antipodes Is. 34 M9
Antlers 42 D7
Antofagasta 48 A2
Anton 42 E3
Antrim 11 B5
Antrim & Newtownabbey □ 11 B5
Antrim, Mts. of 11 A5
Antsirabe 29 H9
Antsiranana 29 G9
Antwerpen 16 C2
Anvers = Antwerpen 16 C2
Anxi 20 C8
Anyang 21 D11
Anzhero-Sudzhensk 18 D9
Ánzio 14 D5
Aomori 22 C7
Aoraki Mount Cook 33 E3
Aosta 12 D7
Aozou, Couloir d' 27 D9
Apache 42 D5
Apache Junction 39 K8
Apalachee B. 43 G13
Apalachicola 43 G12
Apalachicola → 43 G12
Apaporis → 46 D5
Apatity 18 C4
Apeldoorn 16 B2
Apia 33 b
Apostle Is. 40 B8
Apostle Islands ⌓ 40 B8
Appalachian Mts. 41 G14
Appennini 14 B4
Appleby-in-Westmorland 8 C5
Appledore 9 F3
Appleton 40 C9
Apure → 46 B5
Apurímac → 46 F4
Aqaba, G. of 27 C12
Aqtaū 18 E6
Aqtöbe 18 D6
Aquitain, Bassin 12 D3
Ar Ramādī 24 C4
Ar Riyāḍ 24 E5
Arab 43 D11
'Arab, Bahr el → 27 G11
Arab, Shatt al → 24 D5
Arabia 3 C13
Arabian Desert = Es Sahrâ' Esh Sharqîya 27 C12
Arabian Gulf = Persian Gulf 24 D6
Arabian Sea 24 F9
Aracaju 47 F11
Aracati 47 D11
Araçatuba 47 H8
Araçuaí 47 G10
Arad 15 A9
Arafura Sea 23 D5
Aragón □ 13 B5
Araguacema 47 E9
Araguaia → 47 E9
Araguari 47 G9
Arak, *Algeria* 26 C6
Arāk, *Iran* 24 C5
Arakan Yoma 25 F14
Aral 18 E7
Aral Sea 18 E7
Aran Is. 11 C2
Aransas Pass 42 H6
Arapahoe 40 E4
Arapiraca 47 E11
Ar'ar 24 C4
Araraquara 47 H9
Ararat, Mt. = Ağrı Dağı 17 C6
Araripe, Chapada do 47 E11
Aras, Rūd-e → 24 A5
Arauca → 46 B5
Araxá 47 G9
Arbīl 24 B4
Arbroath 10 E6
Arbuckle 38 G2
Arcachon 12 D3
Arcadia, *Fla., U.S.A.* 43 H14
Arcadia, *La., U.S.A.* 42 E8
Arcata 38 F1
Arches △ 38 G9
Arco 38 E7
Arctic Bay 37 B11
Arctic Ocean 6 B17
Ardabīl 24 B5
Ardee 11 C5
Ardenne 16 D2
Arderin 11 C4
Ardivachar Pt. 10 D1
Ardmore 42 D6
Ardnamurchan, Pt. of 10 E2
Ardnave Pt. 10 F2
Ardrossan 10 F4
Ards & North Down □ 11 B6
Ards Pen. 11 B6
Arecibo 45 d
Arena, Pt. 38 G2
Arendal 7 F5
Arequipa 46 G4
Arezzo 14 C4
Argentan 12 B3
Argentina ■ 48 D3
Argentino, L. 48 G2
Argostoli 15 E9
Arguello, Pt. 39 J3
Argun → 21 A13
Argyle, L. 30 D4
Argyll & Bute □ 10 E3
Ariana 27 A8
Arica 46 G4
Arinos → 46 F7
Aripuanã → 46 E6
Arisaig 10 E3
Arizona □ 39 J8
Arkadelphia 42 D8
Arkaig, L. 10 E3
Arkansas □ 42 D8
Arkansas → 42 E9
Arkansas City 40 G5
Arkhangelsk 18 C5
Arklow 11 D5
Arles 12 E6
Arlington, *Oreg., U.S.A.* 38 D3
Arlington, *S. Dak., U.S.A.* 40 C5
Arlington, *Tex., U.S.A.* 42 E6
Arlington, *Va., U.S.A.* 41 F15
Arlington, *Wash., U.S.A.* 38 B2
Arlington Heights 40 D10
Arlon 16 D2
Armagh 11 B5
Armagh, Banbridge & Craigavon □ 11 B5
Armavir 17 A6
Armenia 46 C3
Armenia ■ 17 B7
Armour 40 D4
Arnaud → 37 D13
Arnett 42 C5
Arnhem 16 C2
Arnhem, C. 30 C6
Arnhem Land 30 C5
Arno → 14 C4
Arnold 8 D6
Arran 10 F3
Arranmore 11 A3
Arras 12 A5
Arrecife 26 C3
Arrow, L. 11 B3
Arroyo Grande 39 J3
Artesia 39 K11
Artigas 48 C5
Artois 12 A5
Artux 20 D4
Artvin 17 B6
Aru, Kepulauan 23 D5
Arua 28 D6
Aruanã 47 F8
Aruba ☑ 45 E11
Arun → 9 G7
Arunachal Pradesh □ 25 D15
Arusha 28 E7
Aruwimi → 28 D4
Arvada, *Colo., U.S.A.* 38 G11
Arvada, *Wyo., U.S.A.* 38 D10
Arvayheer 20 B9
Arviat 36 C10
Arxan 21 B12
Arzamas 18 D5
As Sulaymānīyah, *Iraq* 24 B5
As Sulaymānīyah, *Si. Arabia* 24 E5
As Suwayq 24 E7
Asahikawa 22 B8
Asamankese 26 G5
Asansol 25 E13
Asbury Park 41 E16
Ascension I. 4 E9
Áscoli Piceno 14 C5
Aseb 24 G4
Asenovgrad 15 C11
Ash Fork 39 J7
Ash Grove 40 G7
Ash Shāriqah 24 D7
Ashbourne 8 D6
Ashburn 43 F13
Ashdown 42 E7
Asheboro 43 D15
Asherton 42 G5
Asheville 43 D13
Ashford 9 F8
Ashgabat 24 B7
Ashington 8 B6
Ashland, *Kans., U.S.A.* 40 G4
Ashland, *Ky., U.S.A.* 41 F12
Ashland, *Maine, U.S.A.* 41 B19
Ashland, *Mont., U.S.A.* 38 D10
Ashland, *Ohio, U.S.A.* 41 E12
Ashland, *Oreg., U.S.A.* 38 E2
Ashland, *Va., U.S.A.* 41 G15
Ashland, *Wis., U.S.A.* 40 B8
Ashley 40 B4
Ashqelon 27 -
Ashtabula 41 E13
Ashton 38 D8
Ashuanipi, L. 37 D13
Asia 3 B14
Asinara 14 D3
'Asīr 24 F4
Asir, Ras 24 G6
Asmera 24 F3
Aspatria 8 C4
Aspen 38 G10
Aspermont 42 E4
Assam □ 25 D14
Assateague Island ⌓ 41 F16
Assen 16 B3
Assiniboia 36 E9
Assiniboine → 36 E10
Assisi 14 C5
Assynt, L. 10 C3
Astana 18 D8
Asti 12 D8
Astipalea 15 F12
Astoria 38 C2
Astrakhan 17 A7
Asturias □ 13 A3
Asunción 48 B5
Aswân 27 D12
Asyût 27 C12
Aṭ Ṭā'if 24 E4
Atacama, Desierto de 48 A3
Atascadero 39 J3
Atatürk Barajı 17 C5
Atbara 27 E12
'Atbara, Nahr → 27 E12
Atchafalaya B. 42 G9
Atchison 40 F6
Athabasca 36 D8
Athabasca → 36 D8
Athabasca, L. 36 D9
Athboy 11 C5
Athenry 11 C3
Athens = Athina 15 F10
Athens, *Ala., U.S.A.* 43 D11
Athens, *Ga., U.S.A.* 43 E13
Athens, *Ohio, U.S.A.* 41 F12
Athens, *Tenn., U.S.A.* 43 D12
Athens, *Tex., U.S.A.* 42 E7
Athina 15 F10
Athlone 11 C4
Atholl, Forest of 10 E5
Athos 15 D11
Athy 11 C5
Atka I. 36 D2
Atkinson 40 D4
Atlanta, *Ga., U.S.A.* 43 E12
Atlanta, *Tex., U.S.A.* 42 E7
Atlantic 40 E6
Atlantic City 41 F16
Atlantic Ocean 2 D8
Atlas Mts. = Haut Atlas 26 B4
Atlin 36 D6
Atmore 43 F11
Atoka 42 D6
Attalla 43 D11
Attawapiskat 37 D11
Attawapiskat → 37 D11
Attica 40 E10
Attleboro 41 E18
Attu I. 36 D1
Atwater 39 H3
Atwood 40 F3
Atyraū 18 E6
Au Sable → 41 C12
Aube → 12 B5
Auburn, *Ala., U.S.A.* 43 E12
Auburn, *Calif., U.S.A.* 38 G3
Auburn, *Ind., U.S.A.* 41 E11
Auburn, *Maine, U.S.A.* 41 C18
Auburn, *N.Y., U.S.A.* 41 D15
Auburn, *Nebr., U.S.A.* 40 E6
Auburndale 43 G14
Aubusson 12 D5
Auch 12 E4
Auchterarder 10 E5
Auchtermuchty 10 E5
Auckland 33 B5
Auckland Is. 34 N8
Aude → 12 E5
Audubon 40 E6
Aughnacloy 11 B5
Augsburg 16 D5
Augusta, *Australia* 30 G2
Augusta, *Ark., U.S.A.* 42 D9
Augusta, *Ga., U.S.A.* 43 E14
Augusta, *Kans., U.S.A.* 40 G5
Augusta, *Maine, U.S.A.* 41 C19
Augusta, *Mont., U.S.A.* 38 C7
Ault 38 F11
Aunis 12 C3
Aurangabad 25 E12
Aurillac 12 D5
Aurora, *Colo., U.S.A.* 38 G11
Aurora, *Ill., U.S.A.* 40 E9
Aurora, *Mo., U.S.A.* 40 G7
Aurora, *Nebr., U.S.A.* 40 E5
Austin, *Minn., U.S.A.* 40 D7
Austin, *Nev., U.S.A.* 38 G5
Austin, *Tex., U.S.A.* 42 F6
Australia ■ 30 E3
Australian Capital Territory □ 32 C4
Austria ■ 16 E7
Autun 12 C6
Auvergne □ 12 D5
Auvergne, Mts. d' 12 D5
Auxerre 12 C5
Ava 40 G7
Avallon 12 C5
Avellaneda 48 C5
Avellino 14 D6
Aversa 14 D6
Avery 38 C6
Aveyron → 12 D4
Aviemore 10 D5
Avignon 12 E6
Ávila 13 B3
Avilés 13 A3
Avoca → 11 D5
Avon →, *Bristol, U.K.* 9 F5
Avon →, *Dorset, U.K.* 9 G6
Avon →, *Warks., U.K.* 9 E5
Avon Park 43 H14
Avonmouth 9 F5
Avranches 12 B3
Awash 24 H4
Awbārī, Idehan 27 C8
Awe, L. 10 E3
Axe → 9 F5
Axel Heiberg I. 37 B11
Axios → 15 D10
Axminster 9 G4
Ayacucho, *Argentina* 48 D5
Ayacucho, *Peru* 46 F4
Ayakkum Hu 20 D6
Aydın 15 F12
Aydingkol Hu 20 C6
Ayers Rock = Uluru 30 F5
Ayeyarwady = Irrawaddy → 25 F15
Aylesbury 9 F7
Aylmer, L. 36 C9
Ayr 10 F4
Ayr → 10 F4
Ayvalık 15 E12
Az Zahrān 24 D6
Az Zāwiyah 27 B8
Azare 26 F8
Azerbaijan ■ 24 A5
Azores = Açores, Is. dos 26 a
Azov 17 A5
Azov, Sea of 17 A5
Aztec 39 H10
Azuero, Pen. de 46 B2
Azul 48 D5

B

Bab el Mandeb 24 G4
Babb 38 B7
Babine L. 36 D7
Bābol 24 B6
Babruysk 18 D3
Babuyan Chan. 23 B4
Bac Lieu 23 C2
Bacabal 47 D10
Bacău 17 A3
Back → 36 C9
Bacolod 23 B4
Bad → 40 C3
Bad Axe 41 D12
Badain Jaran Shamo 20 C9
Badajoz 13 C2
Badalona 13 B7
Baden-Württemberg □ 16 D4
Badlands 40 D2
Badlands △ 40 D2
Baffin B. 37 B13
Baffin I. 37 C12
Bafoulabé 26 F3
Bafoussam 26 G8
Bafra 17 B5
Bagamoyo 28 F7
Bagé 48 C6
Bagenalstown 11 D5
Baggs 38 F10
Baghdād 24 C4
Baghlān 24 C9
Bago 25 F15
Baguio 23 B4
Bahamas, The ■ 45 C10
Bahawalpur 25 D10
Bahía = Salvador 47 F11
Bahia □ 47 F10
Bahía Blanca 48 D4
Bahir Dar 24 G3
Bahrain ■ 24 D6
Baia Mare 17 A2
Baicheng 21 B13
Baie-Comeau 37 E13
Baie Verte 37 E14
Baikal, L. = Baykal, Oz. 19 D11
Bainbridge 43 F12
Baja, Pta. 44 B1
Baja California 44 A1
Baker, *Calif., U.S.A.* 39 J5
Baker, *Mont., U.S.A.* 38 C11
Baker, L. 36 C10
Baker, Mt. 38 B3
Baker City 38 D5
Baker I. 31 A15
Baker Lake 36 C8
Bakers Dozen Is. 37 D12
Bakersfield 39 J4
Bakhmut 17 A5
Bākhtarān = Kermānshāh 24 C5
Bakı 17 B7
Bakony 16 E8
Baku = Bakı 17 B7
Bala 8 E4
Bala, L. 8 E4
Balabac Str. 23 C3
Balaklava 17 B4
Balakovo 18 D5
Balaton 16 E8
Balbi, Mt. 31 B10
Balbina, Represa de 46 D7
Balbriggan 11 C5
Balcarce 48 D5
Balcones Escarpment 42 G5
Bald Knob 42 D9
Baldwin 41 D11
Baldy Peak 39 K9
Baleares, Is. 13 C7
Baleine → 37 D13
Baleshare 10 D1
Bali 23 D3
Balıkeşir 15 E12
Balikpapan 23 D3
Balkan Mts. = Stara Planina 15 C10
Balkanabat 18 F6
Ballachulish 10 E3
Ballaghaderreen 11 C3
Ballarat 32 C3
Ballari 25 F11
Ballater 10 D5
Ballina 11 B2
Ballinasloe 11 C3
Ballinrobe 11 C2
Ballinskelligs B. 11 E1
Ballybunion 11 D2
Ballycastle 11 A5
Ballyclare 11 B5
Ballyhaunis 11 C3
Ballymena 11 B5
Ballymoney 11 A5
Ballymote 11 B3
Ballynahinch 11 B6
Ballyquintin Pt. 11 B6
Ballyshannon 11 B3
Balmorhea 42 F3
Balqash Köli 18 E8
Balsas → 44 D4
Bălţi 17 A3
Baltic Sea 7 F7
Baltimore, *Ireland* 11 E2
Baltimore, *U.S.A.* 41 F15
Baluchistan □ 24 D9
Bam 24 D7
Bamako 26 F4
Bambari 28 C4
Bamberg, *Germany* 16 D5
Bamberg, *U.S.A.* 43 E14
Bamburgh 8 B6
Bamenda 28 C2
Banaba 34 H8
Bananal, I. do 47 F8
Banaras = Varanasi 25 D12
Banbridge 11 B5
Banbury 9 E6
Banchory 10 D6
Banda, Kepulauan 23 D4
Banda Aceh 23 C1
Banda Sea 23 D4
Bandar-e Abbās 24 D7
Bandar Lampung 23 D2
Bandar Seri Begawan 23 C3
Bandırma 15 D13
Bandon 11 E3
Bandon → 11 E3
Bandundu 28 E3
Bandung 23 D2
Banes 45 C9
Banff, *Canada* 36 D8
Banff, *U.K.* 10 D6
Bangalore 25 G11
Bangassou 28 D4
Banggai, Kepulauan 23 D4
Banghāzī 27 B10
Bangka 23 D2
Bangkok 23 B2
Bangladesh ■ 25 E14
Bangor, *Down, U.K.* 11 B6
Bangor, *Gwynedd, U.K.* 8 D3
Bangor, *U.S.A.* 41 C19
Bangui 28 D3
Bangweulu, L. 28 G6
Bani 45 D10
Banja Luka 14 B7
Banjarmasin 23 D3
Banjul 26 F2
Banks I. 36 B7
Banks Is. 31 C12
Bann → 11 A5
Banning 39 K5
Bannockburn 10 E5
Banská Bystrica 16 D9
Bantry 11 E2
Bantry B. 11 E2
Banyak, Kepulauan 23 C1
Banyuwangi 23 D3
Bao'an 21 a
Baoding 21 D12
Baoji 20 E10
Baoshan 20 F8
Baotou 21 C11
Bar Harbor 41 C19
Bar-le-Duc 12 B6
Baraboo 40 D9
Baracoa 45 C10
Baraga 40 B9
Barahona 45 D10
Barakaldo 13 A4
Baranavichy 18 D3
Baranof I. 36 D6
Barataria B. 43 G10
Barbacena 47 H10
Barbados ■ 45 g
Barberton 41 E13
Barbourville 41 G12
Barcelona, *Spain* 13 B7
Barcelona, *Venezuela* 46 A6
Barceloneta 45 d
Bardiyah 27 B10
Bardsey I. 8 E3
Bardstown 41 G11
Bareilly 25 D11
Barents Sea 6 B8
Bari 14 D7
Barinas 46 B4
Baring, C. 36 C8
Barisal 25 E14
Barkley, L. 43 C10
Barkly Tableland 30 D6
Barlee, L. 30 F2
Barletta 14 D7
Barmer 25 D10
Barnard Castle 8 C6
Barnaul 18 D9
Barnesville, *Ga., U.S.A.* 43 E12
Barnesville, *Minn., U.S.A.* 40 B5
Barnet □ 9 F7
Barnhart 42 F4
Barnsley 8 D6
Barnstable 41 E18
Barnstaple 9 F3
Barnwell 43 E14
Baroda = Vadodara 25 E10
Barotseland 29 H4
Barqa 27 C10
Barques, Pt. Aux 41 C12
Barquisimeto 46 A5
Barra, *Brazil* 47 F10
Barra, *U.K.* 10 E1
Barra, Sd. of 10 D1
Barra do Corda 47 E9
Barra Hd. 10 E1
Barrancabermeja 46 B4
Barranquilla 46 A4
Barre 41 C17
Barreiras 47 F10
Barreiro 13 C1
Barretos 47 H9
Barrie 37 E12
Barron 40 C8
Barrow 36 B4
Barrow → 11 D5
Barrow-in-Furness 8 C4
Barry 9 F4
Barstow 39 J5
Bartlesville 42 C7
Bartlett 43 D10
Barton upon Humber 8 D7
Bartow 43 H14
Barú, Volcan 45 F8
Baruun Urt 21 B11
Barysaw 17 C9
Basel 12 C7
Bashkortostan □ 18 D6
Basilan I. 23 C4
Basildon 9 F8
Basin 38 D9
Basingstoke 9 F6
Basle = Basel 12 C7
Basque Provinces = País Vasco □ 13 A4
Basra = Al Başrah 24 C5
Bass Str. 32 C4
Bassas da India 29 J7
Basse-Pointe 44 c
Basse-Terre 44 b
Basses, Pte. des 44 b
Basseterre 45 D12
Bassett 40 D4
Bastia 12 E8
Bastrop, *La., U.S.A.* 42 E9
Bastrop, *Tex., U.S.A.* 42 F6
Bata 28 D1
Batabanó, G. de 45 C8
Batangas 23 B4
Batavia 41 D14
Batdambang 23 B2
Batesburg-Leesville 43 E14
Batesville, *Ark., U.S.A.* 42 D9
Batesville, *Miss., U.S.A.* 43 D10
Batesville, *Tex., U.S.A.* 42 G5
Bath, *U.K.* 9 F5
Bath, *Maine, U.S.A.* 41 D19
Bath, *N.Y., U.S.A.* 41 D15
Bathsheba 45 g
Bathurst, *Australia* 32 B4
Bathurst, *Canada* 37 E13
Bathurst, C. 36 B7
Bathurst I. 37 B11
Bathurst Inlet 36 C9
Batman 17 C6
Batna 26 A7
Baton Rouge 42 F9
Batticaloa 25 H12
Battle 9 G8
Battle Creek 41 D11
Battle Ground 38 D2
Battle Lake 40 B6
Battle Mountain 38 F5
Batu, Kepulauan 23 D1
Batu Pahat 23 C2
Batumi 17 B6
Baudette 40 A6
Bauru 47 H9
Bavaria = Bayern □ 16 D6
Baxley 43 F13
Baxter 40 B6
Baxter Springs 40 G6
Baxter State ⌓ 41 B19
Bay City, *Mich., U.S.A.* 41 D12
Bay City, *Tex., U.S.A.* 42 G7
Bay Minette 43 F11
Bay St. Louis 43 F10
Bay Springs 43 F10
Bayamo 45 C9
Bayamón 45 d
Bayan Har Shan 20 E8
Bayan Obo 21 C10
Bayard, *N. Mex., U.S.A.* 39 K9
Bayard, *Nebr., U.S.A.* 40 E2
Baydhabo 24 J4
Bayern □ 16 D6
Bayeux 12 B3
Bayfield 40 B8
Baykal, Oz. 19 D11
Bayonne 12 E3
Bayrūt 17 D5
Baytown 42 G7
Beach 40 B2
Beachy Hd. 9 G8
Beacon 41 E17
Beagle, Canal 48 H3
Beals Cr. → 42 E4
Bear I. 11 E2
Bear L. 38 F8
Beardmore Glacier 6 F15
Beardstown 40 E8
Béarn 12 E3
Bearpaw Mts. 38 B9
Beatrice 40 E5
Beatty 39 H5
Beauce, Plaine de la 12 B4
Beaufort, *N.C., U.S.A.* 43 D16
Beaufort, *S.C., U.S.A.* 43 E14
Beaufort Sea 6 B18
Beaufort West 29 L4
Beauly 10 D4
Beauly → 10 D4
Beaumaris 8 D3
Beaumont 42 F7
Beaune 12 C6
Beauvais 12 B5
Beaver, *Okla., U.S.A.* 42 C4
Beaver, *Utah, U.S.A.* 38 G7
Beaver →, *Canada* 36 D9
Beaver →, *U.S.A.* 42 C5
Beaver City 40 E4
Beaver Creek 36 C5
Beaver Dam 40 D9
Beaver Falls 41 E13
Beaver I. 41 C11
Beavercreek 41 F12
Beaverton 38 D2
Beawar 25 D10
Bécancour 41 B17
Beccles 9 E9
Béchar 26 B5
Beckley 41 G13
Bedford, *U.K.* 9 E7
Bedford, *Ind., U.S.A.* 40 F10
Bedford, *Iowa, U.S.A.* 40 E6
Bedford, *Va., U.S.A.* 41 G14
Bedford □ 9 E7
Beef I. 45 e
Beeston 8 E6
Beeville 42 G6
Bei Jiang → 21 G11
Bei Shan 20 C8
Bei'an 21 B14
Beihai 21 G10
Beijing 21 D12
Beira 29 H6
Beirut = Bayrūt 17 D5
Beitbridge 29 J6
Béja 27 A7
Bejaïa 26 A7
Bela 24 D9
Belarus ■ 7 G9
Belau = Palau ■ 23 C5
Belcher Chan. 37 B10
Belcher Is. 37 D12
Beledweyne 24 J5
Belém 47 D9
Belen 39 J10
Belep, Îs. 31 D11
Belfast, *U.K.* 11 B6
Belfast, *U.S.A.* 41 C19
Belfast L. 11 B6
Belfield 40 B2
Belfort 12 C7
Belfry 38 D9
Belgium ■ 16 C2
Belgorod 18 D4
Belgrade = Beograd 15 B9
Belgrade 38 D8
Belhaven 43 D16
Belitung 23 D2
Belize ■ 44 D7
Belize City 44 D7
Bell Peninsula 37 C11
Bell Ville 48 C4
Bella Coola 36 D7
Bellaire 41 E13
Belle Fourche 40 C2
Belle Glade 43 H14
Belle-Île 12 C2
Belle Isle 37 D14
Belle Isle, Str. of 37 D14
Belle Plaine 40 E7
Bellefontaine 41 E12
Bellefonte 41 E15
Belleplaine 45 g
Belleville, *Canada* 37 E12
Belleville, *Ill., U.S.A.* 40 F9
Belleville, *Kans., U.S.A.* 40 F5
Bellevue, *Idaho, U.S.A.* 38 E6
Bellevue, *Nebr., U.S.A.* 40 E6
Bellevue, *Wash., U.S.A.* 38 C2
Bellingham 38 B2
Bellingshausen Sea 6 D3
Bellinzona 12 C8
Bello 46 B3
Bellows Falls 41 D17
Belmonte 47 G11
Belmopan 44 D7
Belmullet 11 B2
Belo Horizonte 47 G10
Beloit, *Kans., U.S.A.* 40 F4
Beloit, *Wis., U.S.A.* 40 D9
Belomorsk 18 C4
Belorussia = Belarus ■ 7 G9
Belovo 18 D9
Beloye, Ozero 18 C4
Beloye More 7 D11
Belpre 41 F13
Belt 38 C8
Belton 42 F6
Belton L. 42 F6
Belturbet 11 B4
Belukha 18 E9
Belvidere 40 D9
Belzoni 43 E9
Bemidji 40 B6
Ben Cruachan 10 E3
Ben Dearg 10 D4
Ben Hope 10 C4
Ben Lawers 10 E4
Ben Lomond 10 E4
Ben Macdhui 10 D5
Ben Mhor 10 D1
Ben More, *Argyll & Bute, U.K.* 10 E2
Ben More, *Stirling, U.K.* 10 E4
Ben More Assynt 10 C4
Ben Nevis 10 E3
Ben Vorlich 10 E4
Ben Wyvis 10 D4
Benares = Varanasi 25 D12
Benavides 42 H5
Benbecula 10 D1
Bend 38 D3
Bendigo 32 C3
Benevento 14 D6
Bengal, Bay of 25 F14
Bengaluru (Bangalore) 25 G11
Bengbu 21 E12
Benghazi = Banghāzī 27 B10
Bengkulu 23 D2
Benguela 29 G2
Beni → 46 F5
Beni Mellal 26 B4
Beni Suef 27 C12
Benidorm 13 C5
Benin ■ 26 G6
Benin, Bight of 26 H6
Benin City 26 G7
Benjamin Constant 46 D4
Benkelman 40 E3
Bennettsville 43 D15
Bennington 41 D18
Benoni 29 K5
Benson, *Ariz., U.S.A.* 39 L8
Benson, *Minn., U.S.A.* 40 C6
Benton, *Ark., U.S.A.* 42 D8
Benton, *Ill., U.S.A.* 40 F9
Benton Harbor 40 D10
Bentonville 42 C7
Benue → 26 G7
Benxi 21 C13
Beograd 15 B9
Beppu 22 G2
Berbera 27 E12
Berbérati 24 G5
Berbice → 28 D3
Berdiansk 46 B7
Berea 17 A5
Berens → 41 G11
Beresford 36 D10
Berezniki 40 D5
Bergamo 18 C5
Bergen 12 D8
Bergerac 7 E5
Berhampur = Brahmapur 25 F12
Bering Sea 36 D2
Bering Strait 36 C3
Berkeley 38 H2
Berkner I. 6 E4
Berkshire Downs 9 F6
Berlin, *Germany* 16 B6
Berlin, *Md., U.S.A.* 41 F16
Berlin, *N.H., U.S.A.* 41 C18
Berlin, *Wis., U.S.A.* 40 D9
Bermejo → 48 B5
Bermuda ☑ 4 C6
Bern 12 C7
Bernalillo 39 J10
Berneray 10 D1
Berry 12 C5
Berryville 42 C8
Berthold 40 A3
Berthoud 38 F11
Bertraghboy B. 11 C2
Berwick 41 E15
Berwick-upon-Tweed 8 B6
Berwyn Mts. 8 E4
Besançon 12 C7
Bessarabiya 17 A3
Bessemer, *Ala., U.S.A.* 43 E11
Bessemer, *Mich., U.S.A.* 40 B8
Bethany, *Mo., U.S.A.* 40 E6
Bethany, *Okla., U.S.A.* 42 D6
Bethel 36 C3
Bethlehem, *S. Africa* 29 K5
Bethlehem, *U.S.A.* 41 E16
Béthune 12 A5
Bettendorf 40 E8
Betws-y-Coed 8 D4
Beulah, *Mich., U.S.A.* 40 C10
Beulah, *N. Dak., U.S.A.* 40 B3
Beverley 8 D7
Beverly Hills, *Calif., U.S.A.* 39 J4
Beverly Hills, *Fla., U.S.A.* 43 G13
Bexhill 9 G8
Beyneu 18 E6
Beypazarı 17 B4
Beyşehir Gölü 17 C4
Béziers 12 E5
Bhagalpur 25 D13
Bharuch 25 E10
Bhavnagar 25 E10
Bhilainagar-Durg 25 E12
Bhima → 25 F11

C

D

E

F

G

H

I

J

N

O

T